FINANCIAL BLOGGING

How to Write Powerful Posts
That Attract Clients

PRAISE FOR FINANCIAL BLOGGING

"Susan Weiner's teachings on how to effectively express your unique thought leadership insights and how to be relevant with your target markets through the written word are invaluable. This will be required reading for our clients!"

—**STEPHANIE SAMMONS**, *Wired Advisor*

"Interested in starting a blog, but daunted by the work involved? Susan's step-by-step guide makes the task manageable. Her chapters on financial industry regulation make this book particularly valuable for financial advisors and RIAs."

—**THERESA HAMACHER**, *NICSA*

"As a financial professional, you may not know where to start when writing for client communications or marketing. Susan Weiner's book shows you where. She also leads you through the entire process of how to write effectively and naturally for your business. I highly recommend her book to anyone interested in using written communication in their business."

—**RUSS THORNTON**, *Wealthcare for Women*

"Financial professionals who read Susan's book—and take her e-course—will reap many benefits. These include spending less time on their posts, communicating more clearly, and getting more responses from clients and potential clients. I can't recommend Susan and her work highly enough."

—**AMY BUTTELL**, *Lake Effect Creative*

"I learned a tremendous amount from this great book about the writing process. Susan has inspired me to mind map a year's worth of blog posts!"

—**ELEANOR BLAYNEY**, *CFP, CFP Board Consumer Advocate*

"Writing blog posts is easier with the techniques in *Financial Blogging: How to Write Powerful Posts That Attract Clients*. The worksheets and resources in the back of the book as well as those woven throughout are invaluable."

—**CATHY CURTIS**, *CFP, Curtis Financial Planning*

FINANCIAL BLOGGING

How to Write Powerful Posts That Attract Clients

SUSAN B. WEINER, CFA

InvestmentWriting.com

Financial Blogging: How to Write Powerful Posts That Attract Clients
© 2013 by Susan B. Weiner. All rights reserved.
Printed in the United States of America.
First Edition

ISBN-13: 978-1484975206
ISBN-10: 1484975200

www.investmentwriting.com

CONTENTS

PREFACE 1

INTRODUCTION 5

CHAPTER 1: *Brainstorming Ideas for Your Financial Blog* 7

CHAPTER 2: *Organize Your Thoughts Before You Write* 17

CHAPTER 3: *Jumpstart Your Reader-Centric Writing* 29

CHAPTER 4: *When Your Draft Needs More Focus* 39

CHAPTER 5: *Light Editing* 47

CHAPTER 6: *Sticking to a Blogging Schedule* 55

CHAPTER 7: *SEC and FINRA Compliance* 59

CHAPTER 8: *Attracting and Managing Blog Comments* 65

CHAPTER 9: *Promoting Your Blog* 71

CHAPTER 10: *Hiring a Ghostblogger* 81

CHAPTER 11: *Keep Improving!* 87

APPENDIX: *Helpful Resources* 89

INDEX 107

"You can't wait for inspiration. You have to go after it with a club."

—Jack London

PREFACE

WHY I'VE WRITTEN THIS BOOK

I am writing this book because I know how you feel when you stare at a blank page. When I started as a staff reporter for a weekly mutual fund newsletter back in the mid-1990s, I couldn't get anything right. I struggled to generate story proposals that would win my editor's approval. Even when my ideas made the cut, they failed to push my readers' hot buttons. Plus, my editor had to make too many stylistic edits to my writing. It was so frustrating.

I couldn't figure out what was wrong because I couldn't see my articles through my readers' eyes. This is a big challenge for financial bloggers, too.

Luckily, my boss hired a seasoned newspaper editor to coach the newsletter's reporters. I grew as a writer as I responded to my coach's questions, especially as I rewrote my stories. By the time I left the newsletter, my editor told me I'd developed a great style. What I learned can help you crack some of the challenges faster than I did.

Feedback from editors and clients continued to refine my writing style. Plus, the discipline of writing hundreds of articles helped. I'm fortunate to have worked for a variety of clients during a career of 20-plus years. I've been an in-house manager of investment-related marketing communications for an institutional investment management firm and a bank-owned asset manager. I've freelanced for consumer and trade publications. My corporate clients include a broad range of investment and wealth management firms as well as their vendors.

Over the years, I've seen many poorly written articles composed by smart people trying to communicate interesting ideas. Many authors repeated the same mistakes. They failed to appeal to their readers' interests. They organized their articles poorly. They got bogged down in wordy paragraphs.

This made me want to teach people to identify these bad habits so they could tame them. The Boston Security Analysts Society, an organization of investment portfolio managers, research analysts, and the like, gave me the opportunity to teach a writing workshop. Eventually, the CFA Institute, a global association of investment professionals, invited me to join its speaker bureau. As a result of this relationship, I've spoken across the United States and Canada about "How to Write Investment Commentary People Will Read." This led to workshops on other kinds of financial writing.

I first focused on blogging when a client asked me to coach him on writing better blog posts. This set me to wondering whether I could teach a class to a group of advisors. That thought inspired my "How to Write Blog Posts People Will Read" class for financial advisors, which made its debut in February 2010.

Real-life financial advisors find my techniques helpful. "Blogging is easier (and more fun!) since I took the class. Highly recommend," said Cathy Curtis of Curtis Financial in Oakland, California, who has contributed to the Morningstar Advisor "Markets and Economy" blog in addition to running a blog on her own website. Russell Dunkin, a prolific blogger for McKinley Carter Wealth Services in Wheeling, West Virginia, said, "Susan does a great job taking you through the writing process—from thinking of ideas to organizing your thoughts, and all the way to best practices for posts that actually work. Don't hesitate to sign up for this class!" Michael Stillman of Cloud Capital in Dallas, Texas, who has published articles in *Registered Rep* magazine, said, "Susan's practical, insightful suggestions—along with her Blog Post Preparation Worksheet—have been incredibly valuable resources."

Even the advisors who aren't blogging found they learned writing techniques that helped them in other parts of their professional life. Here's what some of them say:

- "The class is great! I'm really getting a huge amount of value—there really is a process to writing."
- "You really helped me with how to organize my thoughts before writing."
- "I liked how you gave us outside-the-box ideas."

This book captures—and expands on—the techniques taught in my class so you can learn the lessons at your convenience.

ACKNOWLEDGEMENTS

I could never have written this book without my husband, Allan, who has always believed in me. My writing group, the Nobscot Niblets, refused to let me put my manuscript aside and offered helpful feedback every step of the way. The wonderful students in my classes on "How to Write Blog Posts People Will Read" and the readers of my *Investment Writing* blog have been good-humored guinea pigs for my ideas and teaching techniques. A much broader community of writers and financial professionals has also offered ongoing inspiration and support.

INTRODUCTION

WHY YOU SHOULD READ THIS BOOK

Blogging has become a "must" for many independent and fee-only financial advisors. It's a great way to build your business by connecting with current and potential clients as well as referral sources. Blogging attracts prospects, media attention, and speaking engagements. It also cements your reputation as a leader in your field. Savvy investment managers, wealth managers, and other financial professionals know blogs are an excellent way to communicate topical information before it gets stale. This deepens your relationships with clients.

But many advisors struggle to create a steady flow of compelling blog posts. This isn't surprising. After all, your professional training focused on helping clients manage their investments or finances. You may have never taken a writing class or written for publication. Don't worry! Help has arrived.

This book will help you conquer the challenge of producing high quality blog posts by following a step-by-step process, including how to:

- Generate and refine ideas for blog posts that will engage your readers
- Organize your thoughts up front so you can write more quickly and effectively
- Edit your writing so it's reader-friendly and appealing
- Spread the word about your blog

WHAT YOU'LL LEARN

Once you complete and apply Chapters 1–5, you'll have a process for writing blog posts.

Chapter 1: Brainstorming Ideas for Your Financial Blog

Chapter 2: Organizing Your Thoughts Before You Write

Chapter 3: Jumpstart Your Reader-Centric Writing

Chapter 4: When Your Draft Needs More Focus

Chapter 5: Light Editing

Chapters 6–11 will help with time management, compliance, and marketing challenges.

Chapter 6: Sticking to a Blogging Schedule

Chapter 7: SEC and FINRA Compliance

Chapter 8: Attracting and Managing Blog Comments

Chapter 9: Promoting Your Blog

Chapter 10: Hiring a Ghostblogger

Chapter 11: Keep Improving!

Work through these 11 chapters and you'll be ready to launch your successful blog. Already writing a blog? By using the techniques in this book, you can improve your return on investment. And what financial professional doesn't like a higher ROI?

Start now, so you can boost your online presence and win new clients!

CHAPTER 1

Brainstorming Ideas For Your Financial Blog

This chapter is for anyone who has ever wondered, "What can I write about?" Perhaps it's easy for you to suggest—or even write—an occasional article, but the idea of producing multiple posts per month throws you into a panic. You'll learn a variety of brainstorming techniques in this chapter.

TECHNIQUE 1: QUESTIONS

You're probably blogging for one of the reasons mentioned by the financial planners, investment managers, wealth managers, and marketers who have taken my class. You want to do the following:

1. Grow your business by connecting with clients, prospects, and referral sources—and perhaps learn more about them through their comments on your blog
2. Drive traffic to your website
3. Enhance your reputation
4. Educate readers

If you pick topics that interest your target audience, you can achieve these four goals. This is why I suggest you listen to the questions that members of your potential audience ask. There's no easier way to learn about the hopes, dreams, and fears that command their attention.

Here are some questions that financial advisors often encounter:

- Is it time to get back into the stock market? Is it time to sell?
- Is now a good time to buy gold/silver/commodities/ the latest trendy investment?
- Why should I pay for financial advice when I can do it myself?
- How can I save on taxes?
- Will I have enough money to pay for my children's college? To retire?

You may think that these topics have been overdone. However, the beauty of a blog is that tailoring your posts to reflect your personality and appeal to the clients your company targets will give you a distinctive twist on these topics. Your readers will feel you're writing specifically for them. After all, the tax concerns of a young couple earning $50,000 in a year are very different from those of a 30-something entrepreneur with all of her wealth tied up in her company, and both differ from a high-earning 55-year-old man with significant stock options.

Your personal style as a writer and as a financial advisor will also make your posts stand out. The topic of "How can I save on taxes?" loses its blandness when you focus on specifics that matter to your readers. This is why it is powerful to answer your clients' and prospective clients' questions in your blog.

TECHNIQUE 2: FILL IN THE BLANKS

You can't always rely on other people to generate ideas for you. But you can fall back on some classic blog post titles to generate ideas. Many writers find the fill-in-the-blanks method helpful. It's best to start with titles that have proven appeal for readers, like the ones below.

Try filling in the blanks to come up with compelling blog post titles:

- Why you need a _____
- The biggest mistake that _____ make
- The five best _____

- Top three ways to _____
- Seven secrets of how to _____
- A better way to _____
- The myth of _____
- How to get _____ for free

For example, you could write about "Why you need a financial planner today," or "The biggest mistake investors make." Titles like these are strong invitations to read.

This list sparks blog post ideas for most people. It also focuses attention on ways to spin the topics to appeal to human nature. After all, everyone wants to satisfy their needs, avoid big mistakes, and enjoy the best of life.

TECHNIQUE 3: YOUR READING

You can find inspiration in your professional and personal reading. On the professional front, *The Wall Street Journal* is a common source of inspiration. When the *Journal* writes about something, your clients, prospects, and referral sources are often curious about your take on it. They may also need help understanding how the topic applies to them.

You can plumb sources beyond *The Wall Street Journal*. Start with your association or industry reading. The CFA Institute's *Financial Analysts Journal* and its magazine often inspire me (see "Blog Post" box). For you, it may be the *Journal of Financial Planning*, brokerage research, *Investment News*, or the *Seeking Alpha* blog. You can use these publications' topics, but make your contribution unique by spinning them toward your readers' interests and level of sophistication.

Your personal reading can help, too. Look at magazine covers to see what they inspire. For example, an *O, The Oprah Magazine* cover sparked a number of ideas for me.

> **Blog Posts Inspired by Industry Reading**
>
> - Roger Ibbotson Attacks Asset Allocation "Folklore"
> - Institutional Plan Sponsors Make Lousy Decisions
> - Strong Words from Editor of Financial Analysts Journal
> - Provocative Quote about Target Date Fund Advisers
> - Pick Young, Small Hedge Funds for Better Returns?
> - Are Buy-Side Analysts Inferior?
> - Annuities Gathering Steam in Professional Journals
>
> *Source: InvestmentWriting.com*

"De-Clutter Your Life! It's time to simplify things—Oprah's starting with her closet," made me think of:

- De-clutter your financial life: Which documents or electronic records do you need to save?
- Simplify your portfolio: Why 10 mutual funds are better than 35
- Simplify your financial life: Let your advisor be your financial and life-planning quarterback
- Can a custom closet really add to your home's resale value? The top three home improvements for making your home more marketable

Take a moment to jot down ideas that this article title (or another one if you have one handy) inspires for you.

TECHNIQUE 4: THINK UNCONVENTIONALLY

Here are more ways to generate unconventional ideas:

- Write about the dark side of a popularly accepted "truth" about your field. For example, the downside of raising the percentage of your portfolio in bonds as you age.
- Write a debate between two people on opposite sides of a timely issue. For example, does it make sense to invest heavily in U.S. stocks?
- Think about the intersection of your passion—it could be sailing, stiletto heels, or anything else—and financial planning. For example, one of my blogging students wrote about how investors should follow the example set by *Seinfeld*'s George Costanza in a specific episode.

TECHNIQUE 5: MIND MAPPING

Mind mapping is a visual brainstorming technique you can use to generate blog post ideas. I'll talk more about mind mapping in later chapters of this book because it can also be used for organizing and editing blog posts.

June Gould sums up mind mapping's appeal in *The Writer in All of Us: Improving Your Writing Through Childhood Memories:*

[Mind mapping] allows associations to flow out and encourages the emergence of themes and patterns. It accepts mistakes, strange associations, and apparent meandering, so it encourages startlingly original perceptions and creative connection making.

Now let's walk through the steps of creating a mind map so you can learn to create your own.

Step 1: Pick a central idea

The first step in mind mapping blog topics is to pick the "big picture" topic or target audience that you'd like to brainstorm. Write it in the middle of the page and draw a circle around it, as in Figure 1.1.

30-Something Parents

Figure 1.1: *Mind Map Central Idea*

The example that we'll follow through four steps is for a financial advisor whose marketing targets parents in their thirties. The term "30-something parents" is the starting point for her effort to list topics for a year's worth of blog posts.

Step 2: Pick your main branches

In Step 2, you pick your mind map's main topics, which I refer to as "branches." If the idea inside your circle is your mind map's tree trunk, then the lines that extend out from it are its branches. To identify your branches, ask yourself, what are the main areas that come to mind when you think of the topic in the center of your circle?

The 30-something blogger selected children, retirement, career, parents, estate planning, home, and typical parents as her main topics (see Figure 1.2 below).

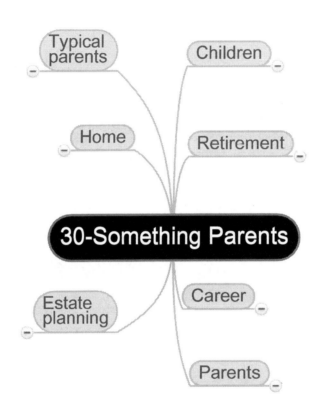

Figure 1.2: *Mind Map with Main Branches*

Step 3: Extend one branch

Let your mind run free in this step and jot down all of the associations from one branch as they occur to you.

The 30-something blogger went from the topic of children to how parents can teach them about various financial topics, so she drew a line from "children" to "how to teach them" and then more lines from "how to teach them" to her three subtopics (see Figure 1.3 below).

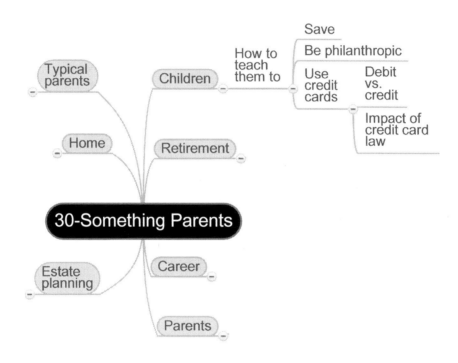

Figure 1.3: *Mind Map with One Branch Extended*

Step 4: Extend more

In Step 4, you extend each of your branches as far out as possible. As each word or phrase inspires a new idea, you diagram it with a new line and words. There's no minimum number of branches or sub-branches or words. You don't even have to graph one branch at a time. Draw your mind map in the order and detail that works for you.

When the advisor completed the mind map, she had enough topics to start her on a year of weekly blogging (see Figure 1.4 below).

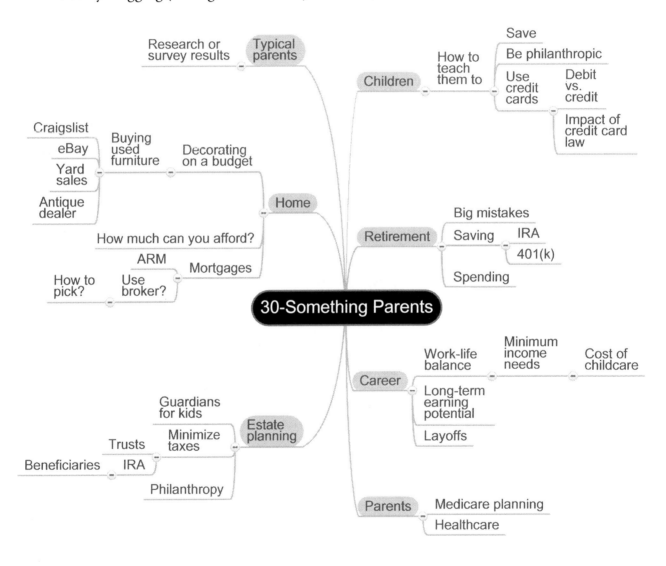

Figure 1.4: *Fully Expanded Mind Map*

USING YOUR COMPUTER

If you prefer brainstorming on your computer or electronic device over working with paper and pencil, you have many options. I'm most familiar with the online mind-mapping site MindMeister.

MindMeister is one of many services that offers a free trial period. Mindomo is another popular choice.

If you're brainstorming with colleagues, an electronic mind map lets you collaborate more easily. Electronic mind maps may also let you record notes on your map and link to related documents and websites.

Still, I often use paper and pencil because it offers me freedom from the computer and its limitations. For example, on paper, I can write at crazy angles and make lines move in any direction I like. I can also vary the size and color of my letters and spill onto another piece of paper—even a flipchart-sized piece of paper. You may find there are times when one method or the other works best. Feel free to switch between the two as it suits you.

WHAT'S NEXT?

After this chapter, you should have a robust list of topics for blogging. The next step is to organize your thoughts before you write.

CHAPTER 2

Organize Your Thoughts Before You Write

"Organizing is what you do before you do something,
so that when you do it, it is not all mixed up."

—A.A. Milne, author of *Winnie-the-Pooh*

When your mind is jumbled, the quality of your writing suffers. This is why I like to organize my thoughts before I write. I organize by identifying my readers and using mind mapping to lay out my information before I hit the keyboard. In addition to describing these techniques in this chapter, I give you a Blog Post Preparation Worksheet so you can capture your insights on paper. When you follow these methods to hone your focus, you can write your blog posts more quickly and concisely.

THE MISSING PIECE—YOUR READERS

Many people pick their topic, then dive into writing. This is a mistake. They're missing an important piece of their puzzle. They're missing their readers—the very reason that financial advisors make the effort to blog.

When you identify, understand, and write for the needs of your readers, it's easier for you to connect with them. This deepens your relationships with clients, attracts prospects and referrals, and builds your reputation as a client-focused advisor.

If you have a blog, focus on the readers you'd like to reach rather than the readers you already have. Identifying your target audience can help you expand your audience in your ideal direction.

Who makes up the ideal audience for your blog? Here are some questions to consider:

1. **How do you define your target market?** One of the students in my financial blogging teleclass had a clear definition: "Upper middle-class, middle-aged professionals with little time, high incomes, and who are overwhelmed with financial issues including budgeting. These people need to make $300,000 per year just to remain cash-flow neutral." Keeping this target readership in mind as you write will make readers feel that you're speaking directly to them. In fact, this will assist in all of your marketing, not only your blog. One advisor told me that until he defined his firm's target this specifically, he felt like he was spinning his wheels.

2. **How sophisticated are your target readers?** You'll use different vocabulary and explain things differently for high school graduates than hedge fund managers. The high school graduate probably won't know what a fund of funds is, whereas a hedge fund manager would feel patronized if you explained the term.

3. **Why do these readers enter into a relationship with you?** For example, are they looking for help with retirement planning? Or are they just starting their careers and trying to manage basic expenses on a tight budget? The answer will help you identify topics for your blog.

4. **What keeps your readers awake at night?** When you play to your readers' hopes and fears, you hook them on your blog. This is especially true if you can solve a problem for them. Perhaps they'd like to save enough money to send their kids to college. Or perhaps they're afraid of losing everything in the stock market's ups and downs. Help them sleep at night and they'll turn to you for advice every time.

WIIFM IS NOT A RADIO STATION

The most common mistake I see in the writing of financial advisors is that they ignore the WIIFM. WIIFM does not represent the call letters of a radio or TV station. Rather, it is short for **W**hat's **I**n **I**t **F**or **M**e. Tell readers how they'll profit from your information so you can command their attention.

Think about your email inbox. When you're pressed for time, how do you prioritize your reading and replies? You probably consider your WIIFM. You'll open emails from your boss or client before a mass email from human resources titled "HR benefits update" because your boss and your clients are more important to you. However, if HR's email touts "Make your pay go further with these new HR benefits," your priorities may change because you see a concrete benefit. Everybody's looking out for himself or herself. Even dedicated humanitarians have a WIIFM. When they read your communications, they're asking themselves, "Can this help me help others?"

Another way of looking at WIIFM is that it represents the benefit that readers will derive from the features of your blog post. I'll demonstrate the difference between features and benefits with two gym ads.

Here's the first ad: "Gym 1 is a premiere fitness, athletics, and rehabilitation facility that features the highest caliber trainers, equipment." Sounds impressive, doesn't it? But those are all merely features. I wonder how many people get excited about gym membership from that ad.

Gym 2's ad says the following:

We've helped our members:
- fit into their clothes
- make their exes jealous
- look amazing at their wedding

Can you see the difference between the two? Gym 2 makes more of an emotional connection with their readers because it focuses on how their gym will help them satisfy their hopes and desires. As American poet Maya Angelou said, "I've learned that people will forget what you said, people will forget what you did, but people will never forget how you made them feel."

Make sure you identify the WIIFM of each blog post before you write it. This will help you engage readers in your blog.

MIND MAPPING TO ORGANIZE YOUR THOUGHTS

WIIFM is one of the points you'll consider when you use mind mapping to collect your thoughts prior to drafting your blog posts. Initially you'll jot down any idea that comes to mind.

Figure 2.1 (next page) is the initial draft of the mind map I created prior to writing a blog post about thank-you notes.

At first, I went through a process similar to that described in Chapter 1. I put my main topic, "Client Thank-You Notes," in the middle. Then I added what I thought would be the main subtopics: cards, handwritten cards, automated cards, target audience, and my recommendations for advisors. I added the target audience branch to force myself to think about the WIIFM. Finally, I took each main branch and traced out the details.

Next, I went through some additional steps. I analyzed the map to find my focus. The two key questions to ask about your map are:

1. **Where's the energy?** In other words, which topics do you feel the most enthusiasm for?
2. **Where's the most data?** Note where you've collected the most material for your post.

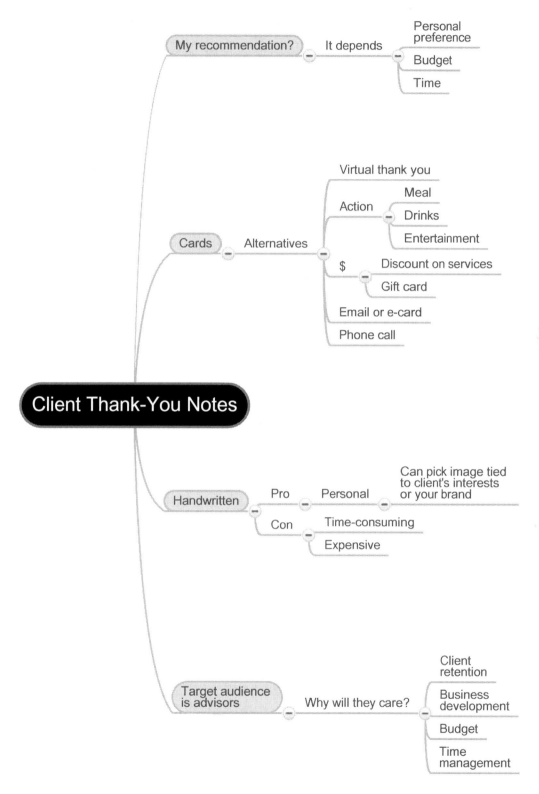

Figure 2.1: *Mind Map for Thank-You Note Blog Post*

I believe energy is more important than data. However, you can't write a compelling blog post if you don't have something to say about your topic.

I've illustrated and explained my thought process in the map on the following page (Figure 2.2). Look first at the area in the big box near the top. This is where my energy focused. It's what I felt most passionately about.

I emphasize finding the energy because I agree with the opinion expressed in the following quote by author Kurt Vonnegut:

> Find a subject you care about and which you in your heart feel others should
> care about. It is this genuine caring, not your games with language, which
> will be the most compelling and seductive element in your style.

Most good blog posts express an opinion or at least give a personal flavor to their subject.

Looking at the boxed area, I realized that my blog post should focus on how to thank clients, rather than on cards. I wouldn't have realized this so quickly without the bird's-eye view of my ideas that was provided by the mind map. One of the big advantages of a mind map over an outline for pre-writing organization of your thoughts is that a mind map can help you discover the flaws in your initial organization. It can also help you identify a better structure. I decided to focus on referrals, one of the most powerful motivations for advisors to thank clients.

When "ways to thank your clients" became the focus, the new subtopics became "cards," "alternatives," and "my recommendations."

I also narrowed my focus to thanking clients for referrals. I decided this partly because blogs pull in the most readers when they're tightly defined. Also, client referrals are a topic of great importance to advisors at any stage of building their businesses. If I could help them win more referrals, I'd appeal to their WIIFM. Speaking of WIIFM, you'll notice that I jotted down "They will care" in the map's lower right corner. For each of your blog topics, it's a good idea to write down the WIIFM for your readers. Otherwise, you run the risk of them surfing right by your post.

As you see in the upper left corner of Figure 2.2, I realized that I didn't have strong feelings about recommending a course of action to advisors. Rather than simply post a wishy-washy conclusion, I decided to poll my blog readers about this topic.

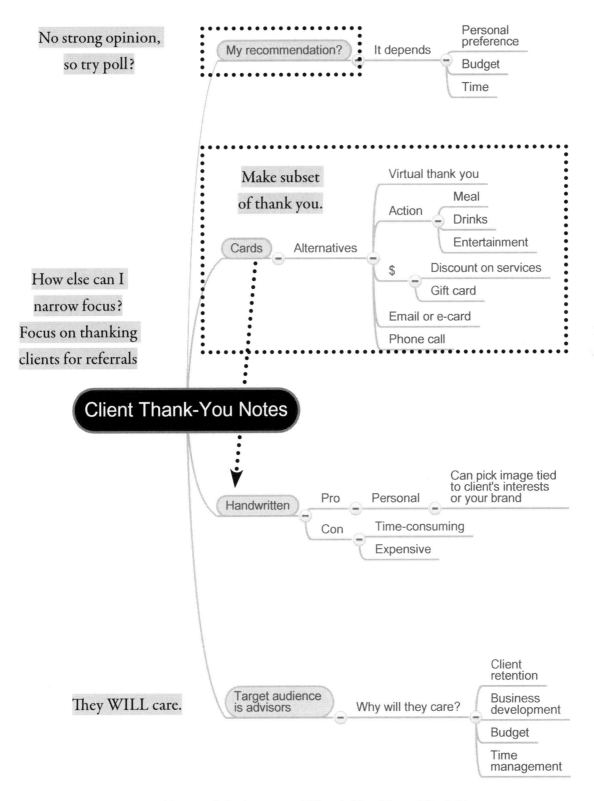

No strong opinion, so try poll?

My recommendation? — It depends — Personal preference / Budget / Time

Make subset of thank you.

How else can I narrow focus?
Focus on thanking clients for referrals

Cards — Alternatives — Action — Virtual thank you / Meal / Drinks / Entertainment

$ — Discount on services / Gift card

Email or e-card

Phone call

Client Thank-You Notes

Handwritten — Pro — Personal — Can pick image tied to client's interests or your brand

Con — Time-consuming / Expensive

They WILL care.

Target audience is advisors — Why will they care? — Client retention / Business development / Budget / Time management

Figure 2.2: *Annotated Thank-You Note Mind Map*

Here's the post that resulted from this exercise:

How should you thank clients for referrals?

Everybody knows you should thank clients when they refer business to you. But financial advisors can't agree on the right way to express their thanks.

Is a verbal thank you at your next client meeting enough? How about adding a card, gift, or discount on your professional services? Often your response depends on the nature of your relationship with the client and the value of their referral.

If you decide on a card, must it be handwritten? Or could you use an automated service such as SendOutCards? I know advisors on both sides of this debate.

Some advisors reward referrals with a discount on their fees. Others shrink from this approach. They feel discounts make clients question the validity of their pricing. The non-discounters may prefer to buy dinner or send a gift to the referral source.

What do YOU think? Express your opinion in the poll you'll find in the right-hand column of this blog. I'll share the results of the poll in my April e-newsletter.

BLOG POST PREPARATION WORKSHEET

If mind mapping doesn't work for you or if you'd like a checklist to ensure your mind map addresses all of your key points, consider using my Blog Post Preparation Worksheet. I provide instructions in the gray shaded area of the form. You write your answers in the empty areas on the right. You'll find a blank worksheet in this book's Appendix.

On the following pages, you'll find a sample of the Blog Post Preparation Worksheet as I would have filled it out for my blog post on thanking clients for referrals.

BLOG POST PREPARATION WORKSHEET

Part One: Who's my reader?

Answer these questions for the specific blog posts that you are writing.

Question	Answer
WHO do you want to reach? Be as specific as possible about your target readers.	*Financial advisors (including financial planners, investment managers, wealth managers, and others who help individuals or organizations meet their financial goals)*
WHAT PROBLEM does this blog post solve for them? What's the benefit to them? Use wording that you think your readers would use.	*How to encourage referrals by thanking clients appropriately when they send referrals—although the post won't provide a one-size-fits-all solution, it will give readers the factors they need to reach a decision*
WHAT SOLUTION will they get from me? For example, a way to reduce costs, ensure secure retirement, save money or time, relieve anxiety.	*Ways to develop business, save time, communicate more effectively*
WHAT'S THE WIIFM (**W**hat's **I**n **I**t **F**or **Me**)?	*Happy clients and more referrals*
Will they understand the technical **VOCABULARY** (AKA jargon) that I use? How educated are they about my topic?	*One term they may not be familiar with is SendOutCards, so I'll provide a link to the SendOutCards website*

BLOG POST PREPARATION WORKSHEET	
Part Two: What's my message?	
Question	Answer
What do I want this blog post to accomplish? Be as narrow as possible. For example: ■ Make the case for including frontier markets in portfolios ■ Show why it's better to invest using a separate account than a mutual fund ■ Explain how brokers have conflicts of interest that plan sponsors may not understand	*I want readers to think about the different ways of thanking clients for referrals, so they can choose the methods that will work best for them.*
What do I want my reader to do? For example: ■ Question whether their current approach to the problem works ■ Recognize themselves in the example I use ■ Contact me	*Answer the related poll that will appear for a limited time in the right-hand column of my blog.*
What's a good **blog post title** that will intrigue the reader and convey the WIIFM (<u>W</u>hat's <u>I</u>n <u>I</u>t <u>F</u>or <u>Me</u>)?	*How should you thank clients for referrals so you can grow your business?*
What are my message's **three main points?**	1. *You must thank clients.* 2. *You have many options.* 3. *The right answer may be specific to you.*
Other important points to remember for this blog post? For example: "My compliance officer won't let me talk about specific mutual funds."	*N/A*

WHAT'S NEXT?

Once you've used the blank worksheet in this
book's Appendix, you'll be ready to tackle
the next step—writing your blog post.

CHAPTER 3:

Jumpstart Your Reader-Centric Writing

You have your blog post topic. You know the main points that you'd like to make. Now it's time to write. In this chapter, we'll discuss two ways to go from ideas to writing: First, freewriting; second, a more structured approach starting from your key point and working through your title and topic sentences. You'll also learn how to make your blog posts reader-centric.

I present two methods so I can appeal to both the right-brained and the left-brained. Right-brained people are intuitive and favor "the big picture." They rely on their gut instincts. However, they may get distracted before they complete their thoughts. Left-brained people are analytical and may get lost in details. It's likely that one of these styles dominates how you approach your blog posts. Freewriting lets the right-brained harness their instincts, while the key-point method puts left-brained analysis before writing. You're most likely to succeed with a process tailored to you because people's minds work differently. Go with the method that works for you. I find both useful, depending on how well I know what I want to write about.

FREEWRITING

Even analytical writers find freewriting helpful when they simply can't think of or decide what to say about a topic.

Follow these steps to start:

1. Pick a subject for freewriting, even if you don't think it will be the actual topic of your blog post.
2. Write non-stop for ten minutes, not bothering to correct typos or revise.

What you write will not be great. However, "It helps you bypass concerns about whether your words sound good or bad. It urges you to write fluently even when you may not feel like it," as June Gould says in *The Writer in All of Us*.

This approach lets your intuitive, creative self run wild without censorship. As Gould suggests, "Don't force your words; just let them flow like a meandering river." A river digs out its main bed, but may also create little streams that don't amount to much. The same is true of freewriting. The key is to use freewriting to identify the river's main bed, so you avoid the little streams in your published blog post.

After you've finished writing, read what you wrote. Now it's time for analysis with a dollop of intuition. Identify what's most interesting and important in your freewritten piece. This will help you figure out what belongs in your blog post. If you have the luxury of time, you may find it easier to analyze your freewriting after a day or two. This lets you distance yourself from your text, so you can read it more as a stranger and less as its creator. In any event, when you find a topic or slant that excites you, your passion will translate into a stronger blog post.

SAMPLE FREEWRITING EXERCISE

Let's look at the freewriting exercise I did to help me figure out how to approach the topic of housing prices. Below you'll find my unedited piece, complete with typos and irrelevant meanderings. Usually I write longhand for this exercise, but I typed this so you can read it.

As you read my poorly written piece below, including typos that are painful for me to read, see if any ideas strike you. Take a minute to jot them down.

Sample Freewriting Exercise (complete with typos)

price of your house. three prices—well really three dollar figures. the list price, which is the price for which the house is for sale. that's the first price that catches your attention. but other prices are important, too. there's in addition to list price there's the assessed value for tax purposes, which may not have any relationship to reality because who knows when the tax guy last came along plus the municipality maynot care that much about the dollar figure as long as they can collect enough texes. and then there's the price that will be set by the appraiser before you finzlize your mortgage. that will have some real-life impact on you. what is the significance of these prices? You need to understand each of them. if you misunderstand any of them, you could make a mistake. let's say you assume the value for tax purposes represents what you should pay. yet that price is out of whack with reality. oops, you're going to pay too much or little for the house.

You probably noticed that my freewriting sample contains many typos and doesn't flow smoothly. But that's okay. Once I'd written it, I scanned through it again to see what was there. The ideas that jumped out at me are in bold.

Freewriting Exercise with Ideas Bolded

*price of your house. **three prices**—well really three dollar figures. the **list price**, which is the price for which the house is for sale. that's the first price that catches your attention. but other prices are important, too. there's in addition to list price there's the **assessed value for tax purposes**, which may not have any relationship to reality because who knows when the tax guy last came along plus the municipality maynot care that much about the dollar figure as long as they can collect enough texes. and then there's the **price that will be set by the appraiser** before you finzlize your mortgage. that will have some real-life impact on you. what is the significance of these prices? You need to understand each of them. if you misunderstand any of them, **you could make a mistake.** let's say you assume the value for tax purposes represents what you should pay. yet that price is out of whack with reality. oops, you're going to pay too much or little for the house.*

The exercise helped me identify key points for my blog post:

- The three different types of valuations placed on a home:
  listing price, tax assessed value, and appraised value
- The possibility of making a mistake

This is just one possible result from this freewriting exercise. For example, if you're a person who has already blogged a lot about housing, you might see in the freewriting key points about the details of tax-assessed value, which could also be the basis for a blog entry.

It's okay to include typos and mistakes in freewriting. You'll type your next draft from scratch as you look at the key points from your analysis.

Try freewriting to see if it works for you. You may find, as one of my blogging students said, "Freewriting is helpful even though seven-eighths of the material isn't usable."

Even if you love freewriting, you should read the sections below on the key-point approach to drafting your blog post. Your post will eventually need to incorporate a key point, a title, and a structure using topic sentences. The difference is that you may identify these items later than the writer who starts with a key-point approach. But don't worry, you'll find techniques to help you with that in the next chapter.

KEY-POINT APPROACH

Another way to start writing your blog post is to identify the key point or opinion that you want to communicate to your readers. Opinions make posts lively. Plus, there's more room for opinions in blogs than in most of your daily communications.

Here's an example of the difference between a key point and a "nobody cares" statement that lacks the power to drive a blog post:

- **Key point**: A blog is essential for financial advisors who want to attract Generation Y clients.
- **"Nobody cares" statement**: The term "blog" is an abbreviation for "web log."

There's no opinion or argument in a "nobody cares" statement. It doesn't call for further discussion because it's a simple fact. Nobody can deny that blog is short for web log. On the other hand, it may be true that a blog is essential for financial advisors who want to attract Generation Y clients, but it's also possible to dispute this.

A key point should also be specific. Here's an example that's too broad: "Written communications are important for financial advisors." True, someone could disagree with this sentence, so it's not a pure "nobody cares" statement. But because it's so generic, this topic is unlikely to attract financial advisors who are seeking to solve a communications problem.

If you don't know your key point, go back to the mind map that you created and analyzed in Chapter 2. This may yield your key point, as it did for me in the earlier example.

YOUR TITLE IS LIKE A HANDSHAKE

You need a title that attracts readers to your blog, with both its appeal to your target audience and an eye to the terms that people type into search engines such as Google, Bing, or Yahoo. The best way to attract attention is by using WIIFM (**W**hat's **I**n **I**t **F**or **M**e), which we discussed in Chapter 2.

A title is like shaking hands on a deal. You promise your reader that they'll obtain a specific benefit from reading.

Let's examine two titles and how we can spice them up. The first title I had to improve was, "Stock Cost-Basis Rules." Doesn't this sound like a topic that your potential clients would skip over? To supercharge it, I asked myself, "Where's the WIIFM?" or "Why should my reader care about this?" These questions inspired my new title, "Save Your Cost-Basis Records or Pay More Taxes Later."

Here's another title I'm sure you've seen, even if you haven't used it yourself: "Report on the First Quarter." It's a common title for quarterly market commentary. The title offers no clue as to whether the commentary is worth reading, or even whether the writer's views change from quarter to quarter or year to year.

Take a minute to jot down some alternative titles for "Report on the First Quarter." To help yourself brainstorm, answer the following questions:

1. Who will care about this topic?
2. What will they care about?
3. Why will they care about it?

When it comes to market commentary, investors are your main audience. They care about what has or will affect their portfolios because this influences whether they can achieve their financial goals as well as other goals that require money.

I suggest tweaking the title of "Report on the First Quarter" to speak to the WIIFM or identify information on which your readers may wish to act. If you're blogging for an audience of large-cap value investors, for example, you could use a title such as "First Quarter Favored Large-Cap Value Investors Like You." If you don't know much about your readers, a forward-looking statement, such as "First Quarter Trends Suggest Market Rally May Stall," might do the trick.

WRITING YOUR INTRODUCTORY PARAGRAPH

Writing a blog post, as poet Maya Angelou says about another topic, "... is like constructing a building: if you start wrong, you'll end wrong." It's important to get your blog post off to a strong start.

Your introductory paragraph, just like your title, should consider the who, what, and why of your blog post. Make sure that your readers feel they have a stake in reading beyond your title and introduction.

Let's look at "before" and "after" versions of the introduction to a blog post about property values.

Before

What's a property worth? It's important to know when you buy or refinance a home. Three different numbers get tossed around—the **listing price**, the **tax assessed value,** and the **appraised value**.

After

What's a property worth? Three different numbers get tossed around—the **listing price**, the **tax assessed value,** and the **appraised value**. If you don't understand the difference between them, you could make a costly mistake when you buy or refinance a home.

Can you see the difference? The "before" version simply says "it's important." The second version raises the stakes—"If you don't understand the difference between them, you could make a costly mistake." It also addresses specific readers, those who are buying or refinancing a house.

In addition to making the reader care about your blog post topic, your introduction should give a good idea of what you're going to cover in your blog post. This establishes a framework so your reader knows what to expect. Clear expectations make for quick, effortless reading. This is especially true when your paragraphs follow your introduction's themes and follow them in the same order.

USING TOPIC SENTENCES TO MAKE IT EASY FOR READERS TO SKIM

Your audience is busy. They're likely to skim your post rather than read it. This is why I recommend strong topic sentences that carry your argument. A topic sentence is usually the first sentence of any paragraph.

Every sentence in a paragraph should support the paragraph's topic sentence. Here's an example of a well structured topic sentence and paragraph.

> As a buyer, you look first at the **listing price** determined by the real estate agent. After all, that's how you figure out if the property is within your reach. Of the three numbers we're considering, it's also the figure with the least methodology behind it. Real estate agents research comparable prices on the Multiple Listing Service, but also listen to their instincts.

When you write strong topic sentences, your audience can grasp the main points of your argument by reading only those sentences. I've highlighted the topic sentences in the example below. Read only the topic sentences on your first pass through the document. Do you feel you get a sense of the overall argument? Next, read the entire article.

> What's a property worth? Three different numbers get tossed around—the **listing price**, the **tax assessed value** and the **appraised value**. If you don't understand the difference between them, you could make a costly mistake when you buy or refinance a home.

> As a buyer, you look first at the **listing price** determined by the real estate agent. After all, that's how you figure out if the property is within your reach.

Of the three numbers we're considering, it's also the figure with the least methodology behind it. Real estate agents research comparable prices on the Multiple Listing Service, but also listen to their instincts.

There's often a big gap between listing price and **tax assessed value**—the dollar amount at which your municipality values your property for taxation. That's to be expected in a rising market for real estate. Why? Because tax assessed values are based on old data. The current tax assessed value of your house was calculated from data collected earlier.

Appraised value is typically the best researched and most current valuation of your property. Banks want to ensure that your property justifies the amount they're lending you. Their appraisers use comparable sales during the last six months. No other 4-bedroom, 1½ bath properties sold nearby recently? No problem; they make specific adjustments for the additional bedroom vs. comparable 3-BR, 1½ bath properties.

Ideally your appraised value should be close to your selling price. If not, you're overpaying or there's something unusual about your transaction.

Did your impression of the topic change dramatically after reading it in full? Probably not.

BUILDING YOUR BLOG POST USING KEY AND MAIN POINTS

When you've identified your one key point, fill in the blanks below.

1. My key point is_____

_____

_____.

Readers will care about it because it solves their problem with_____

_____

_____

_____.

If you can't come up with a reason your readers will care about your key point, then it's not a true key point.

2. The three main points that will prove my key point are:

a. _____

_____

b. _____

_____

c. _____

_____

You don't have to limit yourself to three points. However, a three-point argument is likely to be concise enough to fit comfortably within the typically short confines of a blog post. A blog post with fewer than three supporting points may seem lightweight.

Once you've filled in the blanks, you're ready to start writing. Your two-part answer to Number 1 will become the core of your introduction. The answers to a, b, and c will become your topic sentences for three paragraphs. Flesh out your explanation of each of these points, remembering that each sentence of every paragraph should relate to its topic sentence.

WHAT'S NEXT?

No matter which technique you use (key-point or freewriting), you're unlikely to produce a perfect blog post with your first draft. The next chapter will take you through the refinement process of editing.

CHAPTER 4

When Your Draft Needs More Focus

Sometimes the first draft of your blog post will be well organized. But other times, like a bucking bronco, your draft is out of control. You need to lasso it before you apply the finishing touches. This chapter will help you impose order on your ideas by reconsidering your desired focus and then analyzing your draft using the "first-sentence check" method.

By the way, it's okay if the organization isn't perfect in your first draft. For many writers, the purpose of the first draft is to get their ideas down so they can organize them. "The best writing is rewriting," as *Elements of Style* author E.B. White said.

"BIG PICTURE" EDITING AND ANALYSIS

If you're a right-brained thinker who favors freewriting, you're more likely to need this big picture editing than a left-brained thinker who creates a key-point framework, as discussed in Chapter 3. This is because, one way or another, a strong blog post eventually demands a logical structure.

It may be hard to see where your key points lie. But you can combine intuition and analysis to figure them out. You'll use intuition first. Then, the first-sentence check will help you recognize and analyze your blog post's current structure. This will help you restructure your post.

STEP 1: RECONSIDER YOUR FOCUS

In this step, you'll rethink what the core of your blog post should be. Why? Because often the process of writing unleashes ideas that weren't in your original mind map or freewriting. You may find a new, improved focus for your post.

Read your blog post out loud. As you read, think about where the energy of your draft lies. I often go with what my gut tells me. Intuition is important.

Another option: Ask someone else to read your post out loud. A student in my blogging class told me, "I heard it differently when it was read out loud by others."

If the energy of your post isn't evident, you can ask the following questions:

1. Does my pulse quicken when I use a specific phrase?
2. Do I repeat a specific opinion or topic?
3. What's the one thing I want my readers to do, feel, or think after they read my post?

Your answers should help you identify your focus. You may find that your energy doesn't focus where you initially thought it did. Your draft may have a "white balloon" that needs to be popped or elevated to the focus of your post (see box "Writing Tip").

Once you decide on the key point of your blog post, write it down. If your schedule permits, set your draft aside for at least several days. This will help you to develop more distance from your draft, which may help you to see organizational flaws that weren't obvious in the excitement of creation.

However, if you're short on time, you can start the more analytical phase of this process.

Writing Tip: Pop the balloon or make it your focus

A stroll I took along San Antonio's River Walk inspired this writing tip because an out-of-place detail grabbed my eye. A white balloon bobbed along the surface of the river. Once I spotted the balloon, I couldn't see anything else. Not the gray stone walls. Not the greens or browns of shrubs and trees. Not the pale blue sky.

Something similar happens to your readers when your blog post, article, or white paper includes details that don't belong there. They get distracted. They can't grasp your "big picture" message, just as I couldn't absorb the River Walk's beauty. You can help your readers by popping your "white balloon" to remove distractions from your main message.

Alternatively, sometimes your draft's "white balloon" is a signal that you should shift your focus to center on the balloon, as I have in this section—and in the photo.

STEP 2: HIGHLIGHT YOUR DRAFT'S STRUCTURE AND TOPICS

You may not really understand what information your first draft conveys to your reader. Highlighting its content using the first-sentence check, as I suggest in this section, will help you gain perspective on your draft. You'll see what you've got from a high vantage point so you don't drown in the words. If there's a gap between your intent and your result, this should be obvious because your intent won't appear in your first sentences. You'll also see whether your draft forms a coherent whole.

FINANCIAL BLOGGING: How to Write Powerful Posts That Attract Clients

The first-sentence check method builds on something you learned in the last chapter: You should write strong topic sentences so your audience can grasp the main points of your argument by reading only those sentences. You can see how this works in the example of a draft below:

What's a property worth? Three different numbers get tossed around—the **listing price**, the **tax assessed value** and the **appraised value**. If you don't understand the difference between them, you could make a costly mistake when you buy or refinance a home.

As a buyer, you zoom in on the **listing price**. After all, that's how you figure out if the property is within your reach. Of the three numbers you're considering, it's also the figure with the least methodology behind it. When determining the listing price, real estate agents research comparable prices on the Multiple Listing Service, but also listen to their instincts.

There's often a big gap between listing price and **tax assessed value**—the dollar amount at which your municipality values your property for taxation. That's to be expected in a rising market for real estate. Why? Because tax assessed values are based on old data. The current tax assessed value of your house was calculated from data collected prior to the current calendar year.

Appraised value is typically the best researched and most current valuation of your property. Banks want to ensure that your property justifies the amount they're lending you. So their appraisers use comparable sales during the last six months. What if no other 4-bedroom, 1½ bath property has sold nearby recently? No problem—they make specific adjustments for the additional bedroom vs. comparable 4-BR, 1½ bath properties.

Ideally your appraised value should be close to your selling price. If not, you're overpaying or there's something odd about your transaction.

To highlight and analyze your draft's structure and focus, follow these steps:

1. **Create a first-sentence-check document that consists solely of your title, headings, and the first sentence of every paragraph.** Below, the original is to the left. I've highlighted on the right the information that you should carry over to your first-sentence-check document.

ORIGINAL:

My favorite blogging technique

If you're a blogger, you've probably struggled to find time to write.

Blogging on vacation

I'm writing this post in black ink on a steno pad. I use a spiral-bound steno pad, so I don't lose pages. My boxy printing and black ink are supposed to make my drafts easy for my typist to decipher. My favorite place to blog—and to develop a warehouse of posts—is on an unplugged vacation.

Blogging offline

I write in ink, double-spacing. This is a plus. I like the slow speed and lack of distractions that come with blogging offline. When I type up a draft, it's too easy to tinker with my text as I go. Tough luck for my tweeps. Any brilliant one-liners will be lost to posterity (or obscurity) as I home in on my blog. Writing offline helps with my focus. It's just me, my ideas, my steno pad, and my pen.

Paper fans

I ran a Facebook poll. The poll asked, "Where's your favorite place to blog?" I was surprised to learn that I'm not alone. I suspect that our numbers will decline as technological changes take place.

FIRST-SENTENCE CHECK:

My favorite blogging technique

First Sentence: If you're a blogger, you've probably struggled to find time to write.
Heading: Blogging on vacation

First Sentence: I'm writing this post in black ink on a steno pad.

Heading: Blogging offline

First Sentence: I write in ink, double-spacing.

First Sentence: Tough luck for my tweeps.

Heading: Paper fans

First Sentence: I ran a Facebook poll.

2. **Analyze your document to see if it summarizes your message. If not, identify the document's weaknesses.** Then, delete irrelevant sections and fill in any gaps. Once you have the right content in place, make sure your title, headings, and topic sentences are strong. Then, consider whether every sentence of each paragraph supports its topic sentence. To better understand how this works, you can read my analysis of the "My favorite blogging technique" draft.

Analysis of "My favorite blogging technique" draft

My favorite blogging technique *[Would convey more if it named the technique.]* If you're a blogger, you've probably struggled to find time to write.

Blogging on vacation

I'm writing this post in black ink on a steno pad. I use a spiral-bound steno pad, so I don't lose pages. My boxy printing and black ink are supposed to make my drafts easy for my typist to decipher. My favorite place to blog—and to develop a warehouse of posts—is on an unplugged vacation. *[The last sentence makes more sense as a topic sentence.]*

Blogging offline

I write in ink, double-spacing. This is a plus. I like the slow speed and lack of distractions that come with blogging offline. When I type up a draft, it's too easy to tinker with my text as I go. *[Either of the last two sentences would make a better first sentence because they relate to blogging offline.]* Tough luck for my tweeps. Any brilliant one-liners will be lost to posterity (or obscurity) as I home in on my blog. Writing offline helps with my focus. *[The preceding sentence should go first because it identifies another reason to blog offline.]* It's just me, my ideas, my steno pad, and my pen.

Paper fans

I ran a Facebook poll. *[The Facebook poll is interesting, but it's not the main point of this paragraph, which focuses on the persistence of writing on paper.]* The poll asked, "Where's your favorite place to blog?" I was surprised to learn that I'm not alone. I suspect that our numbers will decline as technological changes take place.

3. **Apply the results of your analysis to revising the blog post.** You can see how I did it by comparing the "before" version of the poorly organized blog post with the better organized "after" version.

<table>
<tr><td align="center">BEFORE</td><td align="center">AFTER</td></tr>
</table>

No batteries required:

My favorite blogging technique

My favorite blogging technique

If you're a blogger, you've probably struggled to find time to write.

If you're a blogger, you've probably struggled to find time to write. Me, too.

Blogging on vacation

Blogging on vacation

I'm writing this post in black ink on a steno pad. I use a spiral-bound steno pad, so I don't lose pages. My boxy printing and black ink are supposed to make my drafts easy for my typist to decipher. My favorite place to blog—and to develop a warehouse of posts—is on an unplugged vacation.

My favorite place to blog—and to develop a warehouse of posts—is on an unplugged vacation. In fact, I'm writing this post in black ink on a steno pad. My boxy printing and black ink are supposed to make my drafts easy for my typist to decipher. I use a spiral-bound steno pad, so I don't lose pages.

Blogging offline

Blogging offline

I write in ink, double-spacing. This is a plus. I like the slow speed and lack of distractions that come with blogging offline. When I type up a draft, it's too easy to tinker with my text as I go. Tough luck for my tweeps. Any brilliant one-liners will be lost to posterity (or obscurity) as I home in on my blog. Writing offline helps with my focus. It's just me, my ideas, my steno pad, and my pen.

I like the slow speed and lack of distractions that come with blogging offline. When I type up a draft, it's too easy to tinker with my text as I go. Writing in ink—even though I double-space to allow for essential corrections—limits my edits. This is a plus. Writing offline helps with my focus. It's just me, my ideas, my steno pad, and my pen. Tough luck for my tweeps. Any brilliant one-liners will be lost to posterity (or obscurity) as I home in on my blog.

Paper fans

I ran a Facebook poll. The poll asked, "Where's your favorite place to blog?" I was surprised to learn that I'm not alone. I suspect that our numbers will decline as technological changes take place.

Paper fans

I was surprised to learn that I'm not alone. I found more paper fans when I ran a Facebook poll on "Where's your favorite place to blog?" I suspect that our numbers will decline as technological changes take hold.

I believe you'll find the "after" version of the blogging post is easier to skim. This is a sign of a well-organized blog post.

WHAT'S NEXT?

Once you've reorganized and rewritten your blog post, you're ready to tweak the little details, such as refining individual sentences. You'll learn how to do that in the next chapter.

CHAPTER 5

Light Editing

Well-written blog posts attract and retain the attention of more readers. Good structure, which we discussed in Chapter 4, isn't enough. You may also need to shorten your sentences and paragraphs.

KEY NUMBERS: 42, 14, AND 2

Shorter is often better. Direct marketers have done studies to see how long-winded you can be before your writing starts to lose readers. Readership drops after you hit the following statistics:

- 42 words per paragraph
- 14 words per sentence
- 2 syllables per word

This is according to research cited in writing workshops by Ann Wylie of Wylie Communications.

These standards are tough to achieve

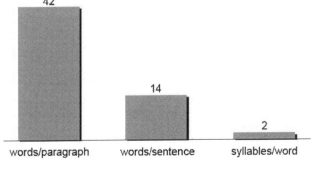

Figure 5.1: *Key Statistics for Writers*

when you write about complex investment or financial planning topics. However, try to tighten your writing by becoming more aware of how your writing compares to these standards. When an individual sentence runs 22 words or more in length, you should look to shorten it. But it's okay if you can't get down to 14. Fourteen isn't always realistic for complex topics.

Microsoft Word users can get exact or approximate counts using the software's readability statistics, as shown in Figure 5.1. Search the "Help" section for "readability statistics" if you don't know how to activate this feature. Other popular word-processing programs also offer this feature.

DO YOU WANT TO BE A 12TH GRADER?

You may think that the higher the grade level of your writing, the better. Your clients are educated and you don't want to offend them, right?

But grade level, as used in the Flesch-Kincaid Grade Level statistic of Figure 5.2, may confuse you. It's better if you think of "grade level" as a measure of how hard you're making readers work to decipher your meaning. A twelfth-grade level means you're making them work as hard as a high school senior. Higher grade levels mean more complex, wordier sentences.

Direct marketers target writing that's eighth grade or lower, which is widely considered to be the reading level at which most American adults can read and comprehend quickly. I aim for tenth grade in my financial articles and sometimes go lower in blog posts.

Becoming aware of your wordiness is more important than hitting a specific word count or grade level. Once you're aware, you can improve your writing by paring back. If you can cut your average sentence length by 10%, you're making progress.

For a quick experiment, drop a paragraph you've written into the Readability

Readability Statistics	? X
Counts	
Words	452
Characters	2154
Paragraphs	17
Sentences	31
Averages	
Sentences per Paragraph	2.5
Words per Sentence	13.5
Characters per Word	4.6
Readability	
Passive Sentences	0%
Flesch Reading Ease	64.4
Flesch-Kincaid Grade Level	7.6
	OK

Figure 5.2: *Readability Statistics from Microsoft Word*

Index Calculator at Standards-Schmandards.com. Hit the "calculate score" button to discover your level. Next, experiment with shortening your sentences. Input the new, shorter versions to see how they affect your grade level.

I agree with William Strunk, who wrote the following in the original edition of *The Elements of Style:*

> Vigorous writing is concise. A sentence should contain no unnecessary words, a paragraph no unnecessary sentences, for the same reason that a drawing should have no unnecessary lines and a machine no unnecessary parts.

HOW TO TRIM THE FAT

In this section, I'll show how you can shorten your sentences to make your text easier to read. I'll illustrate my suggestions with "before" and "after" examples.

Eliminate forms of "to be"

When you eliminate forms of the verb "to be," you shorten your sentences. That's not all. Often you'll invigorate them with more powerful verbs, as in the following example.

BEFORE: Inflation was rising rapidly, which was inflicting pain on bond holders.

AFTER: Rapidly rising inflation hurt bond holders.

Use active verbs

Financial writers sometimes hide behind passive verbs when they feel uncertain about a cause-effect relationship. Be aware that passive verbs sap the strength of your writing.

Shifting from a passive verb to an active verb shortens your sentence and makes the cause-effect relationship more evident, as in the following example. This is because an active verb requires that the subject of the verb takes action.

BEFORE: The stock market was affected by the Fed's cut in the fed funds rate.

AFTER: The Fed's cut in the interest rate drove the stock market higher.

Kill adverbs

Instead of Shakespeare's "Kill all the lawyers," I say, "Kill all the adverbs." Adverbs, which modify verbs, usually don't add much to a sentence. I've underlined the adverbs in the following example, in case you don't recognize them. (The "before" sentence is so fat, I couldn't resist deleting more than just the adverbs. You'll see two versions below.)

BEFORE: Today's banking system has morphed into something <u>entirely</u> different and <u>inherently</u> more risky.

AFTER #1: Today's banking system has morphed into a different, riskier system.

AFTER #2: Today's banking system is riskier.

I like author Mark Twain's approach to adverbs: "Substitute 'damn' every time you're inclined to write 'very'; your editor will delete it and the writing will be just as it should be."

Twain extends a similar approach to adjectives: "When you catch an adjective, kill it." Most financial blog posts would benefit from such violence.

HOW TO ANALYZE COMPLEX SENTENCES

Now let's tackle longer sentences. I'm going to show you a process that breaks your analysis and editing into easy steps. But first, let's look at a sentence that's crying out for an "axe."

ORIGINAL SENTENCE: With only two more Fed meetings remaining in 2007 (on Oct. 31 and Dec. 11), the issue remains whether the Fed's unexpectedly aggressive 50 basis point cut in the fed funds rate last week was intended to shock the markets to restore confidence or they are concerned that the underlying economic conditions are worse than most of us think.

This is a l-o-n-g sentence. It's 59 words. Remember, the direct marketers suggest your entire paragraph should run no longer than 42 words, with a limit of 14 words per sentence.

Do you have an idea of how you'd cut this sentence? If not, don't worry. It'll become more obvious after you go through the following steps with a printout of the sentence:

1. Underline the information that's essential to the sentence.
2. Cross out what's not essential.

Here's my take on the essential, highlighted for your reading ease.

ORIGINAL SENTENCE WITH <u>ESSENTIAL</u> ELEMENTS HIGHLIGHTED:
With only two more Fed meetings remaining in 2007 (on Oct. 31 and Dec. 11), the issue remains whether the Fed's unexpectedly aggressive 50 basis point cut in the fed funds rate last week was intended to shock the markets to restore confidence or they are concerned that the underlying economic conditions are worse than most of us think.

ORIGINAL SENTENCE WITH <u>NON-ESSENTIAL</u> ELEMENTS CROSSED OUT:
~~With only two more Fed meetings remaining in 2007 (on Oct. 31 and Dec. 11),~~ the issue remains whether the Fed's ~~unexpectedly~~ aggressive 50 basis point cut in the fed funds rate last week was intended ~~to shock the markets~~ to restore confidence or they are concerned that the underlying economic conditions are worse than most of us think.

This combined analysis below shows what your new sentence should emphasize—the elements highlighted—and the crossed-out elements that it should delete.

ORIGINAL SENTENCE WITH BOTH ESSENTIAL AND NON-ESSENTIAL ELEMENTS MARKED:
~~With only two more Fed meetings remaining in 2007 (on Oct. 31 and Dec. 11),~~ the issue remains whether the Fed's ~~unexpectedly~~ aggressive 50 basis point cut in the fed funds rate last week was intended to ~~shock the markets~~ to restore confidence or they are concerned that the underlying economic conditions are worse than most of us think.

This analysis helped me to streamline the original.

NEW VERSION: The meaning of the Fed's half-percent cut in short-term interest rates is not clear. The Fed may have made this large cut to restore confidence. Or, the Fed may be worried that the economy is in worse shape than most of us think.

As you can see, the new version is shorter, yet it conveys the essential information from the original sentence. In fact, the new version conveys that information more effectively because it strips away the unnecessary information, such as the dates of the remaining Fed meetings. If the author has something to say about those dates, then he or she should move that information lower in the blog post, so it doesn't distract from the most important information.

You can also adopt two more techniques I used with this sentence. First, divide long sentences into two or more sentences. I turned one sentence into three.

Second, eliminate jargon when you address a non-specialist audience. "Basis point" is a great term for bond geeks, but it confuses the heck out of the general public. So "one-half percent" or "0.5%" is better than "50 basis points." The same goes for "fed funds rate," which I replaced with "short-term interest rates."

Jargon is a sore spot for many Americans. "Nearly three-fourths of the 1,203 adults polled said their auto mechanic uses clearer English than their financial professionals," according to a 2008 article by Cathie Gandel in *AARP Bulletin Today*.

When you find jargon in your blog post draft, you have three options:

1. **Substitute a word that's more commonly understood**, such as "short-term interest rates" for "fed funds rate."

2. **Explain**. When you write for both professional and general audiences, you could define terms as you go. For example: "exogenous trends, meaning trends outside the market." In cases like this, shorter isn't always better. Opt for clear communication over achieving a shorter sentence length.

3. **Link to a glossary** that explains the term. People will only click if they need the information; those who know what the term means can skip over the link.

However, you will avoid jargon completely if you use the Warren Buffett approach to writing.

> Write with a specific person in mind. When writing Berkshire Hathaway's annual report, I pretend that I'm talking to my sisters. . . . They will understand plain English, but jargon may puzzle them.

Buffett said this in *A Plain English Handbook: How to Create Clear SEC Disclosure*

Documents, which is a great, free resource for financial writers.

To jog your memory about these techniques, please consult the Blog Post Review Checklist in the Appendix.

WHAT'S NEXT?

If you follow the rules discussed in this chapter, your blog post will emerge shorter and stronger from the editing process. You'll have the mechanics in place to produce worthy postings on a regular schedule, as discussed in the next chapter.

CHAPTER 6

Sticking to a Blogging Schedule

You've probably seen financial bloggers who start strong, and then blog only intermittently, if at all. They fail to achieve the investment or wealth management professional's goal of connecting with clients, prospects, and referral sources. As the saying goes, "80 percent of success is just showing up." Blog regularly and you're bound to see results over the long run. Be patient.

Let's assume that you've got a great line-up of blog topics for the year ahead. After all, you've mastered the brainstorming, writing, and editing techniques in Chapters 1–5. However, you still may have problems posting on a regular schedule. Consider the techniques listed below.

TIP 1: WRITE POSTS THAT ARE "EVERGREEN" OR TIED TO A FUTURE EVENT

That way, you'll have material to post when you're too busy to write. "Evergreen" articles aren't time-sensitive. Like pine trees, evergreen topics don't lose their attractiveness with the changing of the seasons.

I scheduled a bunch of evergreens to run for a two-week period when I was distracted by attending the CFA Institute's annual conference and going on vacation.

Blog posts tied to events such as the April 15 tax deadline or the August-September "back to school" season aren't evergreen. But they can be written and scheduled long before a timely date for posting.

TIP 2: "SET IT AND FORGET IT"

Most blogging platforms allow you to schedule blog posts in advance. This lets you put your blog on autopilot when you're busy. Evergreen posts are perfect for this. When I participated in a Blogathon that required daily posts, I learned how to take automation one step further. I set HootSuite to tweet my blog posts without human intervention. Read about "How to Add an RSS Feed" using HootSuite.

TIP 3: BLOG WHEN THE SPIRIT MOVES YOU

Whether or not your schedule requires you to post, it's much easier to blog when you're in the mood. When I'm there, on a good day I can push out three or more blog posts. To help me write regardless of location, I always carry a spiral-bound notebook or pad of paper. If you prefer electronic methods, type or record notes into your smartphone. Some bloggers swear by software like Evernote to capture information for posts. It's worthwhile jotting down blog ideas, not only full-fledged posts. It's much easier to blog when you don't face a blank computer screen or piece of paper.

TIP 4: SCHEDULE A REGULAR TIME TO BLOG

This tip contradicts the tip above. But different people respond best to different structures. For example, if you're blogging weekly, you may enjoy making a ritual of blogging on Fridays as a reward for getting through your week.

TIP 5: CREATE AN EDITORIAL CALENDAR

An editorial calendar is a list of topics and the dates on which they'll appear on your blog. Topics may be seasonal, like the April 15 tax deadline discussed in Tip 1. Another approach is to identify key words for your blog—such as investments, estate planning, economy, and retirement. You can then cycle through these topics on a regular basis. In the "Monthly Editorial Calendar" example, the blog covers topics related to children in week 1, career in week 2, retirement in week 3, estate planning in week 4, and a diverse set of topics when the month has a fifth week.

Monthly Editorial Calendar

Week	Topic
1	Children
2	Career
3	Retirement
4	Estate Planning
5	January: Guest blogger re: home decorating on a budget
	February: No Week 5
	March: Last-minute tax moves that will save you money on April 15

TIP 6: FIND A BLOGGING BUDDY

Some bloggers find it helpful to be accountable—or to vie in a friendly rivalry—with another blogger. This is especially true if both bloggers post with similar frequency. Find a blogging buddy. It doesn't have to be someone in the financial world. Set goals with your buddy and report to each other on a regular, predetermined basis.

TIP 7: BRING IN A GUEST BLOGGER

You can't cover every single topic of interest to your readers. As a result, guest bloggers may boost your blog's appeal to your target audience and attract fans of your guest. They also relieve some of the pressure on you to meet deadlines week after week.

TIP 8: KEEP IT SHORT

Short blog posts are okay. A 300-word piece will often suffice. You could go as short as 100 words occasionally. Just pick one point and explain it. Having trouble writing in so few words about your topic? Slice it narrower. For example, don't tackle all defined contribution plans in one post. Instead, focus on how moderate-income teachers within 10 years of retirement can invest their 403(b) plans.

TIP 9: RESPOND TO ONLINE ARTICLES OR BLOG POSTS

Notice when you have strong feelings upon reading something. Your passion makes it easier for you to jot down a quick blog post that links to the original article. Links spare you the need to describe the other author's position in detail. However, it's kind to your reader to briefly summarize what sparked your blog post.

TIP 10: HIRE SOMEONE TO TYPE YOUR BLOG POSTS

If you dictate or write your drafts on paper, someone else can input them. After I drafted some posts on a plane, I scanned them for my assistant to type. Another solution is to use voice-recognition software to type your first draft. Dragon Naturally Speaking is a well-known option.

WHAT'S NEXT?

Different techniques work for different people at different times. Find what works for you and stick to it. If you find yourself running out of steam, come back to this chapter to try something new.

CHAPTER 7

SEC and FINRA Compliance

Compliance matters. Your business can be derailed if you run afoul of regulators or your company's compliance professionals. Registered investment advisors (RIAs) fall under the Securities and Exchange Commission (SEC) or their state's securities regulators, which are relatively liberal in their guidance compared to the Financial Industry Regulatory Authority (FINRA), the organization that oversees registered representatives. In addition, be aware of the rules imposed by your employer or broker-dealer.

Regulations and their enforcement are always changing as regulators struggle to keep up with new developments and the political climate for financial communications. Plus, they're subject to interpretation. My main recommendation: When in doubt about compliance issues, ask a compliance professional.

Here are some general guidelines that I'll explore in greater detail below, in addition to suggesting some resources you can tap for information on compliance regulations and practices.

1. Develop guidelines for your content.
2. If necessary, develop an approval process, or submit your content for review by your company's compliance professionals.
3. Save your blog posts in a manner that's easily accessible.

DEVELOP CONTENT GUIDELINES

Compliance can complicate your content. There aren't many black-and-white rules about what you may or may not discuss. FINRA typically goes into more detail than the SEC, as you will see in the last section of this chapter called "Keep up on the latest developments."

In addition, we all know there are things we can mention, but they require tons of disclosures or "qualifier words," such as "may" or "could," which makes it seem as if even we don't believe what we're saying (see "Find the Happy Medium" box). For example, any discussion of specific mutual funds is likely to require extensive disclosures, particularly if you are including performance history for specific periods. If you're subject to FINRA rules, discussions of mutual funds will also require prior approval from your broker-dealer and filing with FINRA's Advertising Regulation department. This is more than most advisors—and blog readers—want to tackle.

Experts on advisor compliance generally say that blogs are considered "retail communications," "advertising," or "marketing materials" for the purpose of compliance, depending on how you use your blog and who regulates your activities. This determines the rules that apply to your blog, at least in the eyes of the regulators. Your employer, broker-dealer, or professional association may impose additional restrictions. For example, the CFA Institute Code of Ethics and Standards of Professional Conduct says, "Members and candidates must not engage in conduct that constitutes a violation of the Code and Standards, even though it may otherwise be legal." Stay up-to-date on all of the relevant organizations' requirements.

If you're an advisor running your own company, I suggest you write guidelines for your blogging. Regulators tend to respond well to written guidelines, especially when you can show that you've developed and followed a systematic process.

Find the Happy Medium

WRONG: I guarantee you a 10% annual return year-after-year if you invest with me.
LEGAL, BUT NOT USEFUL: I have no idea how much your portfolio will return if you invest with me.
BALANCED: I believe a well-diversified portfolio using multiple kinds of investments is the best solution for investors.

Here's what you might include in your blog guidelines:

1. **Topics you'll cover**, along with a list of any disclosures or disclaimers these may trigger—for example, if you're an RIA, will you discuss specific funds or will you keep your discussion at the level of asset classes? It's generally accepted that you should not offer specific advice to specific individuals on your blog. Compliance professionals and regulators are leery of any apparent guarantees. Use phrases such as "we believe"—or "I believe" if you're a solo practitioner—to set off statements that are opinion rather than fact.

2. **Topics you'll avoid**, even though they're of interest, because regulators frown on them—like the SEC and client testimonials—or that require more legal jargon than you prefer.

3. **Disclosures** you'll put on your blog's home page, the footer that runs along the bottom of every page, or elsewhere.

4. **Other practices to reduce regulatory or legal risks**—for example, source documentation, copyright, and blog comment policies.

5. **Approval, filing, and record-keeping requirements** that may apply to you or your firm, such as approvals you may need from your employer or broker-dealer, and record-keeping requirements under applicable SEC rules.

Any data in your blog posts should have a reputable source. For reputable, think Morningstar or Standard & Poor's rather than some random website. It's always best to name the source in your blog post. Linking to the source is also useful, assuming there's no content on the linked page that the regulators might find questionable or misleading.

Beware of copyright infringement. You can't simply copy an article and then say it's okay because you've credited the author and original publication. Unless you receive permission from the copyright holder, you can only reproduce a portion of an article, assuming your excerpt also meets the "fair use" test. The University of Minnesota has a good online tool, "Thinking Through Fair Use," to help you assess whether a court would consider your excerpt to be "fair use."

Decide whether your blog will accept comments, which I discuss in more detail in Chapter 9. Comments are a great way to deepen your relationships with clients and prospects. However, they also expose you to legal risks that may be only partly offset by disclaimers on your blog. You will need to monitor comments for content that is not acceptable to the regulators. For example, what if someone comments with an ad for a Ponzi scheme? I know advisors who have disabled their blogs' comment feature for this reason.

DEVELOP AN APPROVAL PROCESS—OR SUBMIT YOUR CONTENT FOR APPROVAL

A blog post approval process is necessary for most advisors other than solo RIAs. This is to ensure that your content is compliant. Even solo RIAs may find it helpful to review their posts using their own guidelines before they hit "publish." If you run your own RIA, you may wish to develop an approval process to reduce your legal risks from posts written by your colleagues or employees. A formal approval process is required by FINRA. Here's how your process might work (see Figure 7.1 below).

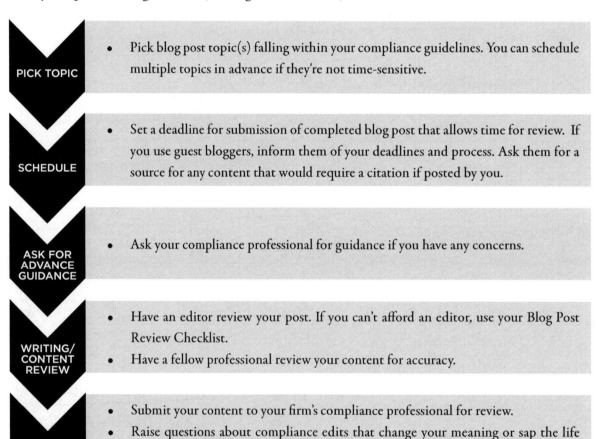

PICK TOPIC
- Pick blog post topic(s) falling within your compliance guidelines. You can schedule multiple topics in advance if they're not time-sensitive.

SCHEDULE
- Set a deadline for submission of completed blog post that allows time for review. If you use guest bloggers, inform them of your deadlines and process. Ask them for a source for any content that would require a citation if posted by you.

ASK FOR ADVANCE GUIDANCE
- Ask your compliance professional for guidance if you have any concerns.

WRITING/ CONTENT REVIEW
- Have an editor review your post. If you can't afford an editor, use your Blog Post Review Checklist.
- Have a fellow professional review your content for accuracy.

COMPLIANCE REVIEW
- Submit your content to your firm's compliance professional for review.
- Raise questions about compliance edits that change your meaning or sap the life from your blog post.

Figure 7.1: *Blog Post Approval Process*

SAVE YOUR BLOG POSTS

FINRA wants you to keep your records—including blog posts and source documentation—for at least three years; the SEC, for at least five years. There are plenty of vendors that provide automated solutions for tracking and archiving your social media, including your blog posts. You'll find some of them in the table of resources in the Appendix. Remember, what's posted on the Internet lasts forever, even if you remove it from your website. When I worked in investment communications for a large asset management company, I had file cabinet after file cabinet filled with documentation of data for my publications. Today you can save sources electronically, but be aware that the SEC has rules about storing electronic records.

KEEP UP ON THE LATEST DEVELOPMENTS

FINRA has several publications relevant to blogging or social media. Here are some titles:

- FINRA Regulatory Notice 11-39 Social Media Websites and the Use of Personal Devices forBusiness Communications: Guidance on Social Networking Websites and BusinessCommunications
- FINRA Regulatory Notice 10-06 Guidance on Blogs and Social Networking Web Sites
- Guide to the Internet for Registered Representatives

The SEC tends to publish less than FINRA. Its most relevant publication is "Investment Adviser Use of Social Media," a *National Examination Risk Alert* published by the SEC's Office of Compliance Inspections and Examinations.

WHAT'S NEXT?

Develop and follow good compliance guidelines for your blogging, and you should be able to blog carefree. All you'll have to worry about then is comments, covered in the next chapter.

CHAPTER 8

Attracting and Managing Blog Comments

Attracting comments and sparking lively conversation is a goal of most bloggers. Comments provide a measure of your success and open a window into your readers' minds. This is why I prefer to allow them. However, comments also pose a compliance challenge for financial advisors who blog. You must decide whether to accept comments before tackling how to attract or manage them.

COMMENTS: YES OR NO?

Comments offer you the opportunity to connect one-on-one with your readers. You gain insight into what stirs them enough that they'll put their thoughts into words. There aren't many other forums that let you interact so freely with prospects and referral sources.

Readers like two-way conversations. They expect you to allow comments on your blog. If you don't, you may seem defensive or uninterested in your readers.

Comments also pose challenges for bloggers, including comments that:

- Spam, selling dubious products or services

- Are mean or inappropriate
- Make requests that the blogger can't satisfy

Comments that raise compliance concerns are a special concern for financial bloggers. These could be positive comments (for example, a client praising the advisor's skills, which violates the SEC rules against investment advisors using testimonials) or negative comments that could be viewed as a "customer complaint." Commenters' recommendations, especially for dubious products, would also be a problem.

Although FINRA has exempted online interactive forums from the pre-approval requirements applicable to "retail communications," they still expect broker-dealers to supervise and review the communications as "correspondence." Because of that, there are still many broker-dealers that don't permit their advisors to have a blog. For those of you who are subject to FINRA's rules, be sure you contact your broker-dealer for approval and restrictions before you create or post to a blog.

WHAT'S AN ADVISOR TO DO?

The easiest response is to turn off the comment feature on your blog. However, if you have the time and resources, enabling comment moderation, along with a spam-blocking plugin, is a good alternative. I discuss these in more detail in the section on managing comments.

ATTRACTING COMMENTS

Writing blog posts that speak to your readers' interests lays the best foundation for attracting reader comments. You also need a critical mass of blog readers. However, you can also use the four techniques listed below to boost your comments.

1. **Ask for 'em.** Invite readers to comment on your posts. Make it easy for them by posing a question at the bottom of your blog post. You can ask for comments in other places, too. Some people send emails or Twitter direct messages asking selected individuals to comment on their posts. This is okay in moderation, but can annoy people when used to excess.

2. **Invite controversy.** When you express strong opinions, you'll find supporters and naysayers. This is likely to lead to comments. For example, quite a few readers commented on my post, "'CFA credential implies a standard of care not always upheld,' says Forbes opinion piece," as I discuss in Chapter 9: Promoting Your Blog.

3. **Ask questions.** Questions are a powerful tool. You can pose questions that your readers care about. You can also ask for their questions about a specific post or a topic, such as retirement planning or saving for college. You'll get more mileage out of your questions if you also post them, along with your blog post, on forums such as LinkedIn Groups, which I discuss in the chapter on promoting your blog.

4. **Respond to comments.** How would you feel if a blogger ignored your comment on her post after you'd gone to the effort of typing it in, entering your contact information, and surviving the spam-blocking test? Not good, right? That's why you should respond to comments, even if it's just to say, "Thank you for commenting."

When commenters list a blog as their website, it's nice if you can find one of their posts to comment on. You never know what good will come of your comments. One potential client contacted me because he'd seen my comment on one of his favorite financial planning blogs.

MANAGING COMMENTS

Here's what I suggest as the basics of managing comments:

1. **Install a spam-blocking plugin.** I use Akismet to stop obvious spam from appearing on my blog. I've also used a comment moderation plug-in, which requires commenters to enter a code before their comment appears. However, the need to enter a code may discourage readers from commenting, especially if the code is difficult to decipher.

2. **Enable comment moderation** if you're concerned about compliance. This means you must approve comments before they appear on your blog. The downside of comment moderation is that it discourages commenters accustomed to the instant gratification of seeing their comments published right away. The trade-off is that you can screen comments for questionable content before they appear on your blog.

3. **Decide how often you'll review comments.** On days that you publish or promote your blog posts, I suggest you pay close attention to comments. If you have enabled comment moderation, it's frustrating for your readers to wait for their comments to appear. You can receive notifications by email so you don't have to visit your blog frequently. If you don't moderate comments, you'll want to respond quickly in case something questionable appears. The SEC says, "A firm may conclude that periodic, daily or real-time monitoring of the postings on a site is appropriate. This determination could depend on the volume and pace of communications posted on a site or the nature of, and the probability to mislead contained in, the subject matter discussed in particular conversation streams" ("Investment Adviser Use of Social Media," *National Examination Risk Alert*, January 4, 2012). You shouldn't let misleading comments linger on your blog.

4. **Set standards for comments.** If you followed my advice in Chapter 8, you set standards for the kind of content you'll allow on your blog. You may need to expand your guidelines to address the special demands of comments. For example:

   - **Will you delete or allow comments that appear to be made solely for the purpose of linking back to the commenter's website?** These comments often compliment your website, but their comments are generic and poorly written. I suspect they're written by robots built for spamming. I delete them.

   - **How will you respond to requests on investment or financial planning situations?** You may wish to prepare a statement about why you can't offer specific advice. You may combine it with generic pointers about the issue raised by the questioner.

- **How will you respond to comments that disagree with or insult you?** Experts recommend acknowledging your commenter's views. This can defuse tense situations. After this, it's up to you whether you'll jump into a debate. Alternatively, you can simply delete comments that offend you. It's your blog, so you set the rules.

5. **Consider adding a disclaimer about comments.** "Many firms post disclaimers directly on their site stating that they do not approve or endorse any third-party communications posted on their site in an attempt to avoid having a third-party posting attributed to the firm," as the SEC noted in "Investment Adviser Use of Social Media," *National Examination Risk Alert* (January 4, 2012). You may sidestep some awkward situations by publishing comment guidelines on your blog. I like the example set by Russell Investments on its *Helping Advisors Blog*. Their main points include the following ideas:

   - They will read every comment, but may not respond to each one.
   - They urge users to stay on topic.
   - They prohibit investment advice from being posted.
   - They require the tone of comments to be respectful.
   - Commenters' email addresses are required for posting; however, Russell states they will not use the emails for any other purpose.

Planning your comment strategy before you start blogging is a good way to boost your blog's visibility and minimize problems along the way.

Speaking of comments, do you have comments on this chapter—or any part of this book? Please send them to me at info@investmentwriting.com. I'm interested in hearing from you.

WHAT'S NEXT?

Once you've created a comment-worthy blog, you should promote it. You'll find ways to do that in the next chapter.

CHAPTER 9

Promoting Your Blog

You've heard this one, I'm sure: "If a tree falls in a forest and no one is around to hear it, does it make a sound?" Similarly, blog posts only make an impression if people read them. This is why you must promote your blog.

You can increase your audience by making your blog's content available in the forms your readers prefer. This may mean posting links in various electronic media and on paper as well as interacting with other bloggers. This makes it easier for search engines and individuals to find you, as I discuss in this chapter.

A client reinforced this lesson for me. She said, "Susan, I love those links you post on LinkedIn!" (see Figure 9.1). I was surprised. This client had declined my offer to send her my e-newsletter, which is the principal way my clients read my blog posts. However, my content developed greater appeal when delivered via one of my status updates on LinkedIn, a medium that suits her style. Linking to blog posts in my LinkedIn status updates was a bigger success than I'd realized because it reached beyond my email list to my LinkedIn connections.

Susan Weiner, CFA

Writing tip: Pop the balloon or make it your focus investmentwriting.com
A stroll along San Antonio's River Walk inspired this writing tip because
an out-of-place detail grabbed my eye.

Like • Comment • Share • 1 second ago

Figure 9.1: *Example of LinkedIn Status Update*

Let's focus on techniques that I've used, including:

- Inserting blog links into other media
- Interacting with others on your blog and their blogs
- Social media distribution and attraction

We'll also touch briefly on search engine optimization (SEO).

INSERTING BLOG LINKS INTO OTHER MEDIA

Start your blog promotion campaign by telling your clients, friends, and referral sources about it. Encourage them to share links to your posts. You'll turn them into fans and promoters of your blog faster than complete strangers.

Some people don't follow blogs or other social media, but they're willing to click on links in an email. You can use your blog posts as the foundation for an e-newsletter to reach them.

Newsletters are a great promotional tool. My blog readership spikes dramatically when I send my monthly e-newsletter, which consists of teaser copy linking to my blog. I insert a short excerpt from the blog post and then offer a clickable link that takes readers to the posting. Plus, Constant Contact, my newsletter program, provides instant feedback on which posts attract the most readers. Other popular e-newsletter platforms include MailChimp, Vertical Response, iContact, and aWeber. Just Google their names to learn more.

Alternatively, you might offer an email subscription or send email announcements to people who are open to receiving your emails.

Some integration techniques involve less work, but they won't draw as many readers either. For example, you can insert your blog's address into your email signature and into "call to action" lines on your website, invoices, white papers, and other documents, with wording such as: "Read my blog post about how to add personality to your writing." This repeat exposure to the message may eventually catch some readers in a receptive mood.

You can get more mileage out of your blog posts by turning them into other documents. You can print them as stand-alone documents for folks who avoid the Internet. Or you can use a series of blog posts as the basis for a white paper. Every year I package my best posts into an e-book of *Investment Writing Top Tips*.

Your blog posts can also form the basis of content in other media. I've turned blog posts into pre-recorded slideshows using SlideShare. You might explore creating podcasts, which are essentially audio recordings that people can download or play from a website. If you're handy with a video camera or webcam, you can create videos of your blog posts and post them to YouTube.

INTERACTING WITH OTHERS ON BLOGS

Remember WIIFM—what's in it for me? Your potential readers and boosters will respond better when you give them a chance to shine on your blog—and when you show your appreciation of their blog posts.

On your blog, you can link to other people's blogs. For example, in the "Looking for inspiration?" section of a blog post (see below), I linked to several blog posts illustrating my point.

Looking for inspiration?

Here are more examples of financial planners who share personal stories:

- In "Never Forget," Jeff Rose of the *Good Financial Cents* blog writes a touching Memorial Day tribute to a fellow soldier.

- "A Bit of Magic—The Beauty of the Human Spirit" by Nathan Gehring of MyFirstFinancialPlanner.com discusses the amazing generosity of a 12-year-old girl whom he encountered at a Financial Planning Association event.

- "My Broken Wife and Your Financial Plan" by Russ Thornton of Wealthcare for Women demonstrates nice use of dialog in his opening. He turns an experience with his wife into a call for his readers to act.

Don't link just for the sake of linking. Find experts or other sources whose subject matter relates to yours. Use quotes or links that strengthen the argument you make in your blog post.

If you have the time, tell the blogger about your link in the comments section of the relevant blog post or tell them about your link via email or social media, if you're connected. However, the blog may automatically alert them to links to their blog or they may monitor links to their blogs using a service such as Google Alerts that notifies them when that blog URL shows up. When they discover your links, they'll probably be curious to visit your blog. If they like what they see, they may stick around.

When readers comment on your posts, you should respond, so they feel heard. At a minimum, say "Thank you for commenting." It's even better if you share your reaction to something they wrote. For example, "I agree with you. I also think that . . ." Another way to appeal to WIIFM is to ask writers who you respect to provide guest posts for your blog and invite them to tell their network about their appearances.

Links from other people's websites to your blog boost your authority. It's not only other people who may be impressed. Search engines also notice. Links from reputable sites that discuss topics related to your blog have the most power to boost your ranking in online searches.

You can also offer incentives to draw readers to your blog. For example, I offer my e-book free to blog readers who take the extra step to subscribe to my e-newsletter, as you see in Figure 9.2.

Receive a free e-book with client communications tips when you sign up for my free monthly newsletter.

Figure 9.2: *Example of Free Offer*

Commenting on other people's blogs is a good way to attract readers. But don't promote yourself or insert a link to your content in the body of your comment. That seems spammy. Instead, join the conversation. Say what you like about the post or raise a question about it. The blogger—and even some of her or his readers—may visit your blog. For example, a prospective client called me after he read a comment I posted on *Nerd's Eye View*, a blog written by influential financial planner Michael Kitces. Be sure to insert the URL for your blog into the "website address" box when you leave your comment, as you see in Figure 9.3.

Figure 9.3:
Insert URL When Commenting

FIND A GUEST-BLOGGING OPPORTUNITY

Appearing as a guest blogger—publishing a post under your byline on someone else's blog—enhances your credibility and broadens your audience. Readers know that reputable sites are discriminating in their choice of guests. As a result, links from these sites boost your search ranking, making you easier to find. When the other blog has a broad audience, it introduces you to many people who might not have found you otherwise.

Some blogs publish their submission guidelines, so you know exactly how to apply to be a guest blogger. Others don't. But there's a simple process you can follow to propose yourself as a featured guest.

Step 1. Study the blog to figure out its audience and focus. Commenting on the blog as you study it will pay off later, if the blogger starts to recognize your name and appreciate your comments and the way that you think and write.

Step 2. Come up with a topic. Your description of your topic should identify the main point you're trying to make and why their readers will care about it.

Step 3. Email the blogger to suggest a guest post. A strong proposal will include the following:

    a. Your understanding of the host blogger's audience and focus

    b. Your topic and why it will appeal to the blog's audience

    c. A brief bio to establish your credibility

    d. Your contact information

It isn't necessary to send your completed blog post right away. In fact, I think it's better not to send it unless requested by the blog owner's submission guidelines.

A proposal lets the blog owner give you suggestions about how to adapt your idea to his or her needs. Assuming you write a good proposal, it also proves that you've read the blog, which boosts the odds that your offer will be accepted.

This may sound like a lot of work, but a well-written inquiry is likely to find a receptive audience. Bloggers are friendly. Plus, they enjoy the breather from writing that your guest post offers.

As you build your network, you'll find guest-blogging opportunities more easily. People will begin to seek you out. Once they've read multiple good posts, they'll assume your post for their blog will be equally good. You won't have as much convincing to do.

SOCIAL MEDIA DISTRIBUTION AND ATTRACTION

Make your blog posts available via social media, such as LinkedIn, Twitter, Facebook, or Google+. You can automate the flow of your blog posts to your social media networks using online tools such as TwitterFeed.com, HootSuite.com, TweetDeck, Seesmic, or NetworkedBlogs.com. HootSuite is the website that helps me to manage my Twitter feeds.

Distribution: Mini case study

Four hundred times—I was thrilled! This is how many times my blog post, "'CFA credential implies a standard of care not always upheld,' says Forbes opinion piece," was posted within a week or so to other social media or emailed, according to my blog's ShareThis widget (a way of making it easy for blog readers to circulate posts).

I couldn't have done it without LinkedIn Groups. I shared this post on three CFA-related LinkedIn Groups, where it generated conversations and clicks (see Figure 9.4).

Here are the lessons I learned:

1. **Sharing your blog posts on LinkedIn Groups can boost visits to your blog**. Four hundred "shares"—distribution of my post via other social media or email—is above average for my blog.

Figure 9.4: *Example of LinkedIn Groups Posting*

2. **A blog post targeted to hot spots of a few LinkedIn Groups can generate more traffic** than a less-targeted post shared with many LinkedIn Groups. My popular post addressed ethics and fiduciary duty—topics that CFA charterholders care a lot about. I suspect that I couldn't have generated another 400 shares by distributing my post to the rest of my 47 LinkedIn Groups. To learn more about LinkedIn Groups, go to learn.linkedin.com/groups.

This kind of broad circulation of blog posts isn't common. But once in a while, your posts will strike a chord with your audience. If you've built your readership and massaged it with savvy use of social media, you can get results like these.

ATTRACT YOUR AUDIENCE WITH CONVERSATION

"Pull" marketing—attracting with lively content tailored to readers' needs—is more powerful than "push"—forcing your content out regardless of reader interest—because members of your target audience will flock to magnetic content made just for them. I've found that raising questions and starting conversations related to my posts can be very effective. It engages readers and invites their responses.

For example, my blog attracts readers who care about quality writing. My "Reader challenge: Rewrite this sentence to make it more powerful" blog post prompted numerous reader comments and shares on my blog and in LinkedIn Groups. It consisted simply of the following text.

This sentence, which was copied from a mutual fund's annual report, cries out for improvement. I'd like to know how YOU would fix it. If you think this sentence is fine as is, you're also welcome to comment.

We thought Best Buy was expensive; however, investors viewed online competitors as presenting a structural issue and Best Buy's valuation declined dramatically during the year.

It's tough to engage in quality conversations on every single social media outlet. Start with one or two that work best for you and your firm. I started with LinkedIn and Twitter, then expanded to Facebook. There are many options to consider, including Google+, YouTube, Tumblr, Pinterest, and others that have yet to be invented.

SEARCH ENGINE OPTIMIZATION (SEO)

Search engine optimization (SEO) is another way of helping readers find your content on the topics that interest them. It's basically the art of figuring out which words your target readers type into search engines to find you, and then using those words skillfully in your blog posts to increase the likelihood you'll be found.

SEO techniques are constantly changing, so do-it-yourselfers need to do ongoing research. Google Webmaster Central provides insights direct from the people who set the rules. There are blogs that focus on SEO such as SEOmoz and Hubspot. To jumpstart your exploration, check out "Top 25 SEO blogs."

You may prefer to delegate your SEO work to a consultant. The people who created your website may also do SEO or give you a good referral.

Step 1: Figure out your keywords

Your keywords may be obvious. Start with your profession, location, and specialty, and spin off from there. If you're a financial planner in the Boston suburb of Waltham who specializes in working with women, you might focus on terms such as:

- Financial planner, financial planning, retirement planning
- Waltham, Massachusetts; Boston; Newton; Belmont; Metrowest Boston
- Financial planner for women, women and money, women's retirement planning

To get ideas for more keywords, use Google Adwords' free keyword tool or one of the many other free or paid tools competing for your attention. Google's tool suggests more terms, such as "certified financial planner," "Boston financial planner," and "wealth manager." It also gives you a sense of how much competition you'll face in attracting people searching for those terms.

"Long-tail keywords"—less popular, more specific keywords—may yield the best results. It would be hard for a new blogger to reach the first page of search engine results for "financial planner." After all, you're competing with financial planners around the world. Moreover, do you really want to attract anyone anywhere who's searching for a financial planner? It's far better to use keywords related to your narrowly defined target audience. That may lead you to long-tail keywords such as "Massachusetts teachers retirement planning."

Step 2: Use keywords skillfully in your post

Write for people, not search engines. I'm so glad that Google itself gives this advice to writers seeking high Google rankings. Even so, there are techniques you can use to make your keywords and blog more visible to search engines.

1. **Put keywords into your blog post titles and headings**. For example, if you're targeting women saving for retirement, you might call a post, "Top Five Retirement Tips for Women Investors."

2. **Use HTML tags wisely**. It seems that search engines give special attention to information between HTML tags, especially the first words inside the tags. HTML tags are codes that identify an element of your webpage and how it should be formatted. For example, a heading tag identifies a heading in the body of your blog post, formatting it so it stands out from the text that follows. Get a savvy blogger to teach you WordPress basics.

3. **Pick your permalinks for impact**. Create a permalink—the URL for an individual blog post—that uses keywords instead of defaulting to numbers to distinguish one post from another. "YourBlog.com/secrets-of-success" will draw more search engine traffic than "YourBlog.com/2350." In WordPress, you can do this in Settings>Permalinks.

4.   **Link to other posts on your blog.** As we discussed in the section on "Interacting with others on blogs," quality links boost your blog posts' credibility with search engines. Another tip: links from within your website also appear to help. Plus, linking to posts on related topics increases the likelihood that people will stay on your blog, exploring other great content and eventually becoming a client. So when you guest-post on another blog, consider including a link to a specific, relevant post—rather than your blog's home page—in the biography that typically appears at the bottom of a guest post.

Step 3: Look at your analytics

Programs such as Google Analytics, a free service at www.google.com/analytics, or JetPack can help you measure what brings readers to your blog. If those topics and techniques turn readers into prospects and referral sources, then it's worthwhile. If posts that aren't central to your business are drawing the most views, then it's time to rethink your strategy.

SEE WHAT WORKS FOR YOU

I've discussed many techniques in this chapter. My best advice? See what works for you and do more of it. What works for me or another advisor won't necessarily work as well for you.

WHAT'S NEXT?

The work that goes into creating and maintaining a blog is extensive, so you may feel you'd like to outsource some of it. In the next chapter, we discuss hiring a ghostblogger.

CHAPTER 10

Hiring a Ghostblogger

Is a ghostwriter right for your blog? Some advisors lack the time or the skill to write persuasively, so they hire someone to do it for them. In this chapter I advise you on how to find and use a skilled writer effectively. However, a ghostblogger—a ghostwriter for your blog—isn't right for everybody, so I also discuss drawbacks and the alternative of hiring an editor.

FINDING A GHOSTBLOGGER

You can save yourself headaches if you decide what kind of ghostblogger you need before you start searching. Ghostbloggers come in many flavors. Some act as reporters, interviewing you and putting your thoughts into words. In this case, you're driving the content. At the other end of the spectrum, some ghostbloggers come up with topics, do research to support a point of view, and then write posts. There are plenty of variations on this theme. Think about which will work best for you.

Key characteristics of ghostbloggers

Depending on how you define your ideal ghostblogger, you should ask about their:

- **Expertise in your field**—Are they completely ignorant of your field, requiring explanation of common technical terms, or are they well-versed in it?

- **Interview skills**—How good are they at zeroing in on essential questions if they interview you to derive content for your posts? Can they use the interview material to write posts that sound as if they're written by you?

- **Research skills**—Can the writer distinguish between respectable and unreliable sources for your field? If not, you may waste tons of time making corrections.

- **Writing skills**—Can the writer convey your ideas clearly and in an interesting manner?

- **Ability to work independently and to meet deadlines**—You've already got lots of work to do. You don't need a writer whom you must coach and nag through every step of the blog post writing process.

Your ghostblogger need not excel in each of these areas. Indeed, depending on your budget, you may find that writers who are strong in every area may be too expensive. You can offset a writer's weaknesses—or make up for a tight budget—by investing more of your own time.

Speaking of budget, at least one financial advisor says she's able to buy usable blog posts at a rate of 10 cents to 25 cents per word (a double-spaced page in a 12-point font runs about 250 words, which is a respectable length for a blog post). I'm skeptical that you'll get quality work for this kind of pay. Rates go up from there, and may easily hit $1 to $2 a word for more experienced writers.

Sources for ghostbloggers

An ideal way to find a ghostblogger is to hire someone who has already written articles, white papers, or other content for you. This means they already understand some of your content. Plus, you both have an idea of whether your working styles are compatible. The next best source is a referral from someone you trust.

Beyond that, there are plenty of websites that offer free or low-cost opportunities to post ads recruiting writers. Some specialize in writers, while others offer a wide array of services. At the low end, there are sites such as online-writing-jobs.com, freelancewriting-gigs.com, CraigsList.com, and oDesk. Please note: I haven't used any of these sites to hire writers, so I can't vouch for them.

If you'd like to hire a journalist, the American Society of Journalists and Authors offers FreelanceWriterSearch.com. You can search a database of writers at Freelance Success, a membership organization in which I participate.

Working with a ghostblogger

The more clearly you define your blog post guidelines to your ghostblogger, the more likely you are to be satisfied with the results. Consider filling out the Blog Post Preparation Worksheet you learned about earlier in this book (see Appendix). Here are a few more things you should specify:

Word count—You can give your writer a range, such as 250–400 words or no more than 500 words. This is especially important if the writer charges you by the word.

Useful background information—This could include articles or websites. Focus. Don't drown your writer in irrelevant data.

Format—Do you want a plain text file or can you handle Microsoft Word documents? If you want your writer to add HTML formatting or drop their blog post into your WordPress blog, you should tell them in advance. Don't assume that's included in your writer's price quote or expertise.

Deadline—Set a due date for the ghostblogger's work. Allow ample time for editing and compliance review.

You now have the information you need to make smart decisions about hiring a ghost-blogger. Even if you end up writing all of your own blog posts, you may be able to apply these tips if you ever outsource larger writing projects.

However, I do recommend that you consider the drawbacks of using a ghostblogger before you hire one.

THE DISADVANTAGES OF USING A GHOSTBLOGGER

Loss of authenticity and the added challenges involving compliance/ethics, cost, and time-liness are the biggest potential minuses when you hire a ghostblogger.

Loss of authenticity

Readers, including clients and prospects, prize blogs partly for the blog's authentic voice. In other words, readers enjoy a glimpse into the writer's personality and passions. Personality and passions are the easiest ways for financial advisors to distinguish themselves from their many competitors with similar credentials and expertise. There's also something that writers call "voice," which is the distinctive way you express yourself. You will lose this authenticity with a ghostblogger who doesn't know you well.

Before you hire a ghostblogger, consider working around your weaknesses as a writer. Have difficulty expressing yourself clearly? Stick with short blog posts that express one opinion. If you link to someone else's articulate article or blog post, you could get away with writing as little as one sentence with your take on the other writer's topic. For example, you could link to an op-ed essay about economic policy and say, "I disagree because of x, y, and z." Concerned about your grammar, spelling, or punctuation? Hire a proofreader. You could even avoid writing by posting an audio or video file to your blog. Of course, this wouldn't relieve you of the need to satisfy compliance requirements.

Compliance and ethics

Registered representatives must disclose their use of ghostbloggers; registered investment advisors' responsibilities aren't as clear.

FINRA's "Misleading Communications About Expertise" (Regulatory Notice 08-27) says, "Registered representatives may not suggest (or encourage others to suggest) that they authored investment-related books, articles or similar publications if they did not write them. Such a publication created by a third-party vendor must disclose that it was prepared either by the third party or for the representative's use."

If the registered rep contributes nothing other than payment for a blog post, he or she can't claim sole credit. An appropriate byline might be "Submitted by Rachel Registered-Rep and written by Glenda Ghostwriter" or "Written for Rachel Registered-Rep by Glenda Ghostwriter," according to an email exchange I had with Paul Tolley, chief compliance officer of Commonwealth Financial Network. There's more leeway when the registered rep contributes ideas and editorial guidance. For example, if someone writes an article on the basis of content and editorial review provided by a rep, the article's byline should include the writer's name in addition to the rep's. "The rep can't claim sole authorship because it's not true," says Tolley. However, a byline such as "By Rachel Registered-Rep with Glenda Ghostwriter" could work, as long as Rachel truly contributed to the writing.

I'm not aware of any laws or regulations governing the use of ghostwriters by registered investment advisors (RIAs). However, "RIAs are fiduciaries that are subject to the anti-fraud provisions of the Investment Advisers Act, and as such they are held to an even higher standard than registered reps," says Tolley, who believes the SEC would likely view ghostwritten material as fraudulent without the appropriate disclosure. If you are not the source of the ideas in a ghostwritten blog post, some people feel you should disclose that, as registered reps must. Indeed, this may be required for CFA charterholders, many of whom are registered investment advisors, under the CFA Institute's Code of Ethics. The ethics of the situation are not as clear if you provide the ideas and someone else does the writing.

Costs measured in money and time

Using a ghostblogger demands an investment of money and time. Fees cover a broad range, depending on the writer's skill and expertise, as I discussed in "Finding a ghostblogger" earlier in this chapter. A relatively inexpensive writer may do fine on non-technical topics, but require time-consuming corrections on technical topics.

Time is also an issue in terms of how quickly blog posts reach your readers. When you write your own blog posts, you can write and publish a post on a hot topic on the same day. When you rely on a ghostblogger, you've got to factor in that person's schedule. For some topics, a day's delay means many lost opportunities for readership.

Be aware of the pros and cons when you hire a ghostblogger. Your blogging experience will go more smoothly as a result.

ANOTHER OPTION: HIRING AN EDITOR OR PROOFREADER

If insecurities about your writing abilities are what drove you to consider a ghostblogger, then you should consider hiring an editor or proofreader. Everyone can benefit from having someone else read their work.

To find an editor or proofreader, use the techniques I described for finding a ghostblogger. Rates for editing and proofreading will typically run somewhat lower than for ghostblogging.

WHAT'S NEXT?

Now that you've got the basics, it's important to put them to use. Keep writing!

CHAPTER 11

Keep Improving!

Congratulations, you've made it through this book! Now you have an overview of how to write blog posts and manage related tasks and challenges in a way that will attract prospects and deepen your relationships with clients and referral sources. As you blog, please keep this book handy to refresh your memory about the lessons most relevant to you.

If you've been applying what you learned as you read this book, you've already made great strides. The good news is: The more you write, the better you will become. As author Jeffrey Carver says in Jon Winokur's *Advice to Writers*:

> Practice, practice, practice writing. . . . You learn by making mistakes and then seeing where you went wrong.

The Carver quotation points to another certainty. You will make mistakes. They could be as small as a typo or as big as targeting your blog at the wrong audience. Typos happen to everyone. You can correct them and move on after refining your Blog Post Review Checklist. As for other mistakes, you can take advantage of the fact that blogs change. As you identify things that don't work, you can experiment with new methods or approaches.

For example, my blog began as a series of brief reports on presentations I saw at the Boston Security Analysts Society (BSAS). Today it's rare that I report on a BSAS meeting or any other public presentation. Instead I share my own spin on effective financial communications—and I have a blast doing it!

You may sometimes feel discouraged, but don't give up! Maybe your posts don't get the comments or social media mentions that you'd like. You can work on that. Writing a blog is a journey. You start in one place and may end up in a totally different place, with detours along the way. The great thing is that your blog will help you to grow as a writer and as a professional. I know that I'm a better writer and communicator as a result of my frequent blogging. You can make the same kind of progress. Your clients and your business will benefit from improved communications.

If you still have questions about any of these topics, please visit my blog at www .investmentwriting.com/blog. You may find your answer there. If not, please post your question, so I can consider it as the topic of a future blog post.

You can also contact me at

- Info@InvestmentWriting.com
- The Investment Writing Facebook page: www.facebook.com/InvestmentWriting
- My Twitter feed: @SusanWeiner

If you're not already blogging, get started now! I look forward to learning about your successes.

APPENDIX

Helpful Resources

For your convenience, I've included some worksheets and other resources in this section.

- Fill-in-the-Blanks Topic Brainstorming Exercise
- Mind Map Components for Brainstorming Blog Post Topics
- Blog Post Preparation Worksheet
- Topic Sentence Analysis
- Readability Statistics
- Blog Post Review Checklist
- Blog Promotion Techniques
- Compliance Resources
- Websites of Resources Cited
- Love the Book? Take the Class

FILL-IN-THE-BLANKS
TOPIC BRAINSTORMING EXERCISE

To generate ideas for blog posts, try filling in the blanks in the following list of blog post titles. For a more detailed explanation of this exercise, see Chapter 1.

- Why you need a _____

- The biggest mistake that _____ make

- The five best _____

- Top three ways to _____

- Seven secrets of how to _____

- A better way to _____

- The myth of _____

- How to get _____ for free

Here are some examples of filled-in titles:

- Why you need a **<u>financial plan</u>**

- The biggest mistake that **<u>new 401(k) contributors</u>** make

- The five best **<u>ways for young parents to save money</u>**

MIND MAP COMPONENTS
FOR BRAINSTORMING BLOG POST TOPICS

See Chapter 1 for detailed instructions on using mind maps to brainstorm blog post topics.

Start with filling in the focus of your blog post.

Center circle:

_____

Then, fill in the branches with the first topics that come to mind. After you've filled in the branches, then fill in each topic that the branch brings to mind.

Branch 1

    a.

    b.

    c.

    d.

Branch 2

    a.

    b.

    c.

    d.

Branch 3

    a.

    b.

    c.

    d.

BLOG POST PREPARATION WORKSHEET

Part One: Who's my reader?
Answer these questions for the specific blog posts that you are writing.

Question	Answer
WHO do you want to reach? Be as specific as possible about your target readers.	
WHAT PROBLEM does this blog post solve for them? What's the benefit to them? Use wording that you think your readers would use.	
WHAT SOLUTION will they get from me? For example, a way to reduce costs, ensure secure retirement, save money or time, relieve anxiety.	
WHAT'S THE WIIFM (**W**hat's **I**n **I**t **F**or **M**e)?	
Will they understand the technical **VOCABULARY** (AKA jargon) that I use? How educated are they about my topic?	

BLOG POST PREPARATION WORKSHEET

Part Two: What's my message?

Question	Answer
What do I want this blog post to accomplish? Be as narrow as possible. For example: ■ Make the case for including frontier markets in portfolios ■ Show why it's better to invest using a separate account than a mutual fund ■ Explain how brokers have conflicts of interest that plan sponsors may not understand	
What do I want my reader to do? For example: ■ Question whether their current approach to the problem works ■ Recognize themselves in the example I use ■ Contact me	
What's a good **blog post title** that will intrigue the reader and convey the WIIFM (<u>W</u>hat's <u>I</u>n <u>I</u>t <u>F</u>or <u>Me</u>)?	
What are my message's **three main points?**	
Other important points to remember for this blog post? For example: "My compliance officer won't let me talk about specific mutual funds."	

TOPIC SENTENCE ANALYSIS

To assess whether your blog post is easy to skim, analyze its structure using the exercise described below and in Chapter 4: When Your Draft Needs More Focus.

1. Write out your title, headings, and the first sentence—the topic sentence—of each paragraph of your blog post.

Title

_____

Heading (Insert where applicable)

_____

Topic Sentence

_____

Heading or Topic Sentence _____

_____

Heading or Topic Sentence _____

_____

Heading or Topic Sentence _____

_____

Heading or Topic Sentence _____

_____

Heading or Topic Sentence _____

_____

2. Read the sentences silently or out loud. Do you get a good sense of the overall argument you make in your blog post? If not, you need to rewrite your article.

3. If your blog post passes the test in #2, then examine each paragraph individually. Read the topic sentence. Then ask yourself, does every sentence in this paragraph support the topic sentence? If not, you may need to delete or move that sentence. Having a hard time figuring out what sentence order works? Put each sentence on a separate line, print them out, cut them up into one sentence per piece of paper, and move them around like puzzle pieces to find the right sequence.

READABILITY STATISTICS

Smart use of your word-processing software's readability statistics can tighten your writing. Use that program to obtain the readability statistics for your first draft. Another alternative is to use the Readability Index Calculator at www.standards-schmandards.com/exhibits/rix.

Record the key statistics for your first draft. These may include:

- Word count: _____
- Sentences per paragraph: _____
- Words per sentence: _____
- Characters per word: _____
- Flesch-Kincaid Grade Level: _____

Next, rewrite your draft, trying to simplify your sentences and languages. Record the key statistics for your second draft, trying to drive your numbers down without sacrificing clarity or flow.

- Word count: _____
- Sentences per paragraph: _____
- Words per sentence: _____
- Characters per word: _____
- Flesch-Kincaid Grade Level: _____

Were you able to make your draft more reader-friendly? The ease with which your readers grasp your message is more important than specific statistics.

BLOG POST REVIEW CHECKLIST	
I have a clear opinion statement.	√

I have included the following in my first paragraph (or high up in my blog post):
  ■ Key-point statement—the main point I'm making in this blog post
  ■ Reason why (also known as WIIFM) this message will interest a specific group of readers	

My title tells the reader what they'll learn about.	
My title is easy to understand.	
My message is clear and tailored to my reader.	√
I summarize my main point in the first sentence or first paragraph.	
I start a new paragraph or new bullet point for each new main point.	
My readers can get the point of my blog post by reading only the first sentence of each paragraph.	
Each sentence of a paragraph supports the paragraph's topic sentence.	
I use headings, if appropriate, to indicate where a new section starts.	
My headings make a point, rather than just listing a topic.	
My points proceed in logical order.	
The tone and level of familiarity is appropriate for my relationship with the reader.	
My reader will understand my vocabulary. I can type "define: *word*" into Google to get a definition that may help explain things better. Some other resources: investopedia.com, www.investorwords.com, www.morningstar.com/InvGlossary, www.wikipedia.org.	
My average sentence length is as short as possible given the complexity of my topic. My goal is an average sentence length of 14 words. I can check using Microsoft Word's Readability Statistics.	
My average paragraph length is 60 words or less. If I use Microsoft Word, I can get an approximate sense of this by multiplying the Readability Statistics' "Words per Sentence" times "Sentences per Paragraph."	
My Flesch-Kincaid Grade Level is 10 or less.	
I use active rather than passive verbs. Microsoft Word's Readability Statistics gives my percentage of passive sentences. For more on active vs. passive, go to: owl.english.purdue .edu/owl/resource/539/01.	

BLOG POST REVIEW CHECKLIST (continued)

	√
I have made good word choices.	

I delete unnecessary phrases:
- as follows
- as such
- in the process of
- _____
- _____

(I've started your checklist with common phrases. Fill in the blank lines with phrases you've identified as problems for you.)

I replace:
- are VERBing —>VERB (replace forms of the word "to be" to create stronger sentences)
- as —> because (for less ambiguity, when appropriate)
- as was the case in —> as in
- in regards to —> about
- on a year-to-date basis —> year-to-date
- time period of April and May —> April and May
- _____
- _____

(Fill in the blank lines with phrases you've identified as problems.)

I use correctly:
- affect vs. effect. "Affect" means to influence, to pretend (verbs); feeling (noun). "Effect" means a result; being in operation (nouns); to make happen (verb).
- Words I often confuse: _____

NOTE: Use the Confusing Words *website to help distinguish between confusing words.*

	√
I have avoided common grammar and punctuation errors.	

Bullet points
- I put a period at the end of each bullet point IF it is a complete, stand-alone sentence. Otherwise, no closing punctuation is required.
- I use parallel construction. For examples, go to owl.english.purdue.edu /owl/resource/623/01.

BLOG POST REVIEW CHECKLIST (continued)

Commas ■ I put a comma before "which," but not "that." For rules about commas, go to owl.english.purdue.edu/owl/resource/607/01.	
Quotation marks ■ I put punctuation inside the closing quotation mark, except for colons, semicolons, and sometimes question marks. For examples, go to owl .english.purdue.edu/owl/resource/577/03.	
USE THIS AREA TO LIST MORE OF YOUR COMMON MISTAKES. You may find it helpful to focus on correcting one bad habit at a time.	
	√
I have used one or more of these proofreading techniques:	√
Reading my blog post out loud	
Having a colleague proofread for me	
Reading it three times to myself	
Reading each sentence individually from the bottom up	
Using Microsoft Word spell-check	
I've made my blog post visually appealing	√
Plenty of white space	
Photos or other images, if appropriate	
Boldface type, if appropriate	

BLOG PROMOTION TECHNIQUES

Which of the following techniques will you use for blog promotion?

_____ Insert blog links and content into other media

_____ Create a newsletter based on your blog

_____ Insert your blog's address into your email signature

_____ Insert your blog's address into "call to action" lines

_____ Print blog posts as stand-alone documents to hand out

_____ Turn a series of blog posts into a white paper or e-book

Interact with others on blogs, while keeping compliance constraints in mind

_____ Link to relevant content on other people's blogs in the body of your blog posts

_____ Mention your link in the comments section of the other person's blog

_____ Respond to others who comment on your blog posts

_____ Comment on relevant blog posts by others

_____ Find a guest-blogging opportunity

_____ Invite others to guest-post on your blog

Social media distribution and attraction

_____ Share your blog posts as status updates on LinkedIn, Twitter, and Facebook

_____ Share your blog posts in LinkedIn Groups and other relevant forums

_____ Start social media conversations on topics related to your blog

_____ Use search engine optimization

_____ Look at your blog analytics and social media interactions, so you can figure out what attracts your target readers

COMPLIANCE RESOURCES

Below, you'll find additional resources to help you keep up on the latest compliance developments. All of the individuals or companies named in the table have commented on social media compliance. I can't vouch for how well they know the compliance constraints that you operate under. Sources are listed in alphabetical order.

Name	Twitter Tag	Blog	Website
Abromovitz, Les	none	none	www.riacomplianceguy.com
Offers compliant content services for websites and advertisements.			
Actiance	@actiance	blog.actiance.com	www.actiance.com
Enables organizations to leverage the safe and productive use of unified communications, collaboration and Web 2.0, including blogs and social networking sites.			
Advisor Tweets	@AdvisorTweets	www.advisortweets.com/blog	www.advisortweets.com
Aggregates the tweets produced by U.S.-based financial advisors using Twitter to advance their business.			
Compliance Building	@DougCornelius	www.compliancebuilding.com	www.compliancebuilding.com
Collects information on compliance issues applicable to real estate private equity firms.			
Erado	@Erado	www.erado.com/blog	www.erado.com
Offers social media compliance.			
Everyday Tenacity	@EverydTenacity	everydaytenacity.com	everydaytenacity.com
Provides original research and perspectives on the asset management/investment management industry and highlights industry trends and news.			
FP Pad	@BillWinterberg	fppad.com	fppad.com
Note: Offers technology insights in the financial planning community.			
Hill Advisors	@cindihill	hilladvisors.wordpress.com	hilladvisors.com
Comprehensive compliance services and solutions for the financial professional who is a registered investment advisor (RIA).			

COMPLIANCE RESOURCES (continued)

Name	Twitter Tag	Blog	Website
RegEd	@RegEdArkovi	RegEd Arkovi	www.RegEd.com
Offers social media archiving and surveillance.			
Relay Station Social Media	@sthepeterson	www.relaystationmedia.com/blog	www.relaystationmedia.com
Helps companies use social media to reach meaningful goals. It provides insight, digital strategy, tactics, and training.			
Rock the Boat Marketing	@RocktheBoatMKTG	www.rocktheboatmarketing.com/blog	www.rocktheboatmarketing.com
Offers reporting, observation and information exchange on issues involving financial services companies and their use of digital media.			
SEC Law	@astarita	seclaw.blogspot.com	www.seclaw.com
News and commentary on the law of the financial markets.			
Smarsh	@SmarshInc	www.smarsh.com/blog	www.smarsh.com
Offers email solutions, message archiving, email hosting, and website production and hosting.			
Socialware	@Socialware	blog.socialware.com	www.socialware.com
Offers platform services for social business management.			
Triplestop	@joepolidoro	www.triplestopllc.com	www.triplestopllc.com
Provides services in social and traditional marketing, development, and online solutions.			
Wealth Management Marketing	@KristenLuke	www.wealthmanagementmarketing.net/resources/blog	www.wealthmanagementmarketing.net
Offers a full spectrum of marketing services for independent Registered Investment Advisory, financial planning, and wealth management firms.			
Wired Advisor	@WiredAdvisor	blog.wiredadvisor.com	www.wiredadvisor.com
Offers blogging, social media, and online marketing solutions.			

WEBSITES OF RESOURCES CITED

You can also find these links on the "Links" page on my *Investment Writing* blog.

Resources	Shortlink	URL
A Plain English Handbook: How to create clear SEC disclosure documents	1.usa.gov /U3gNMC	sec.gov/pdf/handbook.pdf
Akismet	bit.ly/Y5sWF0	www.akismet.com
"CFA credential implies a standard of care not always upheld," says Forbes opinion piece	bit.ly/TlsSQr	investmentwriting.com/blog/2010/08 /cfa-credential-implies-a-standard- of-care-not-always-upheld- says-forbes-opinion-piece
ConfusingWords.com	bit.ly/Rlbdry	www.confusingwords.com
Financial Analysts Journal	cfa.is/P9HQbR	www.cfapubs.org/loi/faj
FINRA Regulatory Notice 10-06 Guidance on Blogs and Social Networking Web Sites	bit.ly/PwQHWx	www.finra.org/Industry/Regulation /Notices/2010/P120760
FINRA Regulatory Notice 11-39 Social Media Websites and the Use of Personal Devices for Business Communications: Guidance on Social Networking Websites and Business Communications	bit.ly/Vu212u	www.finra.org/web/groups /industry/@ip/@reg/@notice /documents/notices/p124186.pdf
Freelance Success	bit.ly/XwU4xa	www.freelancesuccess .com/findawriter.php
FreelanceWriterSearch.com	bit.ly/SHGpPX	www.freelancewritersearch.com
Google Adwords	bit.ly/R8xncQ	adwords.google.com
Google Alerts	bit.ly/Rof45v	www.google.com/alerts
Google Analytics	bit.ly/Y5vD9p	www.google.com/analytics
Google Webmaster Help	bit.ly/17I5rcH	www.youtube.com /GoogleWebmasterHelp

WEBSITES CITED (Continued)

Website	Shortlink	URL
Guide to the Internet for Registered Representatives	bit.ly/P9NGtO	www.finra.org/Industry/Issues /Advertising/p006118
Helping Advisors Blog	bit.ly/UOK9DN	blog.helpingadvisors.com /comment-guidelines
"How to Add an RSS Feed" using HootSuite	bit.ly/Tlm1Xj	help.hootsuite.com /entries/144073-how-to-add-an-rss-feed
How to Add Personality and Warmth to Your Financial Writing	bit.ly/SnRffz	investmentwriting.com/blog/2012/06 /how-to-add-personality-and-warmth- to-your-financial-writing-part-one
How to Write Blog Posts People Will Read: A Five-Lesson Class for Financial Advisors	bit.ly/TIDhrJ	investmentwriting.com /learn-to-write-better /speeches-and-workshops/blog-writing
Hubspot	bit.ly/Vu7uWN	blog.hubspot.com/blog
Investment Adviser Use of Social Media	1.usa.gov/P9NL0D	www.sec.gov/about/offices/ocie /riskalert-socialmedia.pdf
Investment News	bit.ly/SHicZU	www.investmentnews.com
***Investment Writing* Blog**	bit.ly/Vu8g6i	www.investmentwriting.com/blog
***Investment Writing* Facebook Page**	on.fb.me /UONUZI	www.facebook.com/InvestmentWriting
InvestmentWriting.com	bit.ly/TIDgE3	investmentwriting.com
Investopedia.com	bit.ly/RofXLy	investopedia.com
InvestorWords.com	bit.ly/PwY4gI	www.investorwords.com
JetPack	bit.ly/S2tcQV	wordpress.org/extend/plugins/jetpack
Journal of Financial Planning	bit.ly/S2fVb2	www.fpanet.org/journal

WEBSITES CITED (Continued)

Website	*Shortlink*	*URL*
Learn about LinkedIn Groups	bit.ly/TIzMkP	learn.linkedin.com/groups
Microsoft Word's Readability Statistics	bit.ly/S1LmC4	office.microsoft.com/en-us /word/HP051896011033.aspx
MindMeister	bit.ly/PVL6Ja	www.mindmeister.com
Mindomo	bit.ly/Ro8P1y	www.mindomo.com
Morningstar Investment Glossary	bit.ly/XwV2tg	www.morningstar.com/InvGlossary
Purdue OWL: Active and Passive Voice	bit.ly/Y5xpHw	owl.english.purdue.edu /owl/resource/539/01
Purdue OWL: Commas	bit.ly/S1MmWO	owl.english.purdue.edu /owl/resource/607/01
Purdue OWL: Parallel Construction	bit.ly/XwWKLo	owl.english.purdue.edu /owl/resource/623/01
Purdue OWL: Quotation Marks	bit.ly/R8zWM6	owl.english.purdue.edu /owl/resource/577/03
Seeking Alpha	bit.ly/Rl2q8W	seekingalpha.com/author/market-blog
SEOmoz	mz.cm/QL4GVo	www.seomoz.org/blog
SlideShare	slidesha.re /WPzNUP	slideshare.net
Standards-Schmandards.com Readability Index Calculator	bit.ly/TllAwj	www.standards-schmandards .com/exhibits/rix
"Thinking Through Fair Use": University of Minnesota	bit.ly/WPskVJ	www.lib.umn.edu/copyright /fairthoughts
"Top 25 SEO Blogs"	bit.ly/TLlVEw	www.dailyblogtips.com /top-25-seo-blogs
The Wall Street Journal	on.wsj.com/P9Hzpi	online.wsj.com/home-page
Wikipedia	bit.ly/QL5Ss7	www.wikipedia.org

LOVE THE BOOK? TAKE THE CLASS

If you enjoyed this book, you're a great candidate to benefit from my hands-on blogging class, "How to Write Blog Posts People Will Read: A Five-Lesson Class for Financial Advisors" (see Blog Writing page on my site).

The class gives you the opportunity to apply the book's lessons. Plus, you get feedback from a seasoned writer—me.

The best learning comes from applying what you read or hear. Visit my website at InvestmentWriting.com to learn more.

Index

active verbs, 49

adverbs, 49–50

approval process, 62

brainstorming, 7. *See also* mind mapping

comments, 61, 65, 74

compliance, *See* approval process, FINRA, SEC

complex sentences, 50

content guidelines, 60–62

editing, "big picture," 39

editorial calendar, 56–57

editors, 86

FINRA, 59

first sentence check, 42–46

focus, 39

freewriting, 30–32

ghostbloggers, 81

guest blogging, 57, 75

key-point approach, 32, 37

keywords, 78–80

linking, 72–75

mind mapping, 10–14, 20–24, 91

paragraphs, 34

posts: checklist, 97–99; editing, 39, 47, 49; evergreen, 55; organizing, 17; preparation worksheet, 25–26, 92–93; saving, 63; scheduling, 55; structure, 41; titling, 33–34; topics, 41

promotion, blog, 71, 100

readability statistics, 47, 96

readership, 17–18

reader-centric writing, 29

SEC, 59

SEO, 78–80

social media, 76

target audience, 18

titles, 33–34

topic sentences, 35, 94

WIIFM (what's in it for me), 19, 20, 22, 25–26, 33–34, 73–74, 92–93, 97

worksheets: blog post preparation, 25–26, 92–93; blog post review checklist, 97–99; fill-in-the-blanks, 8–9, 90; key point, 37; appendix with all worksheets, 89–100

"Keep it simple. Be clear. Think of your reader, not yourself."

—Roger Angell

About Susan Weiner, CFA

SUSAN WEINER, CFA, helps financial professionals like you increase the impact of your writing. She writes and edits articles, white papers, investment commentary, web pages, and other communications for leading investment and wealth management firms. Her *Investment Writing* blog is popular with advisors who care about writing that deepens their connections with clients and prospects.

Susan first taught "How to Write Blog Posts People Will Read" in 2010. She has spoken on "How to Write Investment Commentary that People Will Read" across the U.S. and Canada for the CFA Institute. Before becoming a freelancer, she was director of investment communications at Columbia Management Group, a trustee at Batterymarch Financial Management, and a staff reporter for a weekly mutual fund publication. She knows how to use language as a financial professional and a journalist.

Articles that Susan has written, edited, or ghostwritten have appeared in *Advisor Perspectives, Boston Globe, Bottom Line/Personal, CFA Magazine, Financial Planning, Louis Rukeyser's Mutual Funds, Wealth Manager*, and other national publications.

GAIN ACCESS TO BONUS CONTENT

You can gain access to bonus content exclusive to book buyers by visiting my website at www.investmentwriting .com/bonuscontent. Simply enter your email address and name in the registration form to gain instant access.

Bonus content includes fillable, saveable PDF files of the Blog Post Preparation Worksheet and the Blog Post Review Checklist as well as email notifications about updates to the book. You will also be added to the free *Investment Writing Update* e-newsletter, if you don't already subscribe at the email address that you use to register.

Made in the USA
Las Vegas, NV
15 March 2021